The Youth Tourist

THE TOURIST EXPERIENCE

Series editor: Richard Sharpley

The Tourist Experience series addresses a notable gap in the literature on Tourism Studies by foregrounding the tourist experience in a cohesive and thematically structured manner.

Taking a novel approach by presenting both short form publications and longer form monographs exploring issues in the tourist experience, the series will seek to build a comprehensive set of texts that collectively contribute to critical discourse and understanding of the contemporary tourist experience. Short form publications will review specific types of tourist by focusing primarily on the influences and nature and significance of their experiences within a socio-cultural framework while longer titles will embrace contemporary empirical and conceptual perspectives and debates as a means of understanding experiences.

Recent volumes:

Un-ravelling Travelling: Emotional Connections and Autoethnography in Travel Research
Sue Beeton

The Adventure Tourist: Being, Knowing, Becoming
Jelena Farkic and Maria Gebbels

The Backpacker Tourist: A Contemporary Perspective
Márcio Ribeiro Martins and Rui Augusto da Costa

The Mindful Tourist: The Power of Presence in Tourism
Uglješa Stankov, Ulrike Gretzel and Viachaslau Filimonau

Forthcoming Volumes:

The Responsible Tourist: Conceptualizations, Expectations and Dilemmas
Dirk Reiser and Volker Rundshagen

The Sport Tourist
Sean James Gammon

The Youth Tourist: Motives, Experiences and Travel Behaviour

BY

ANNA IRIMIÁS
Corvinus University of Budapest, Hungary

United Kingdom – North America – Japan – India – Malaysia – China

Emerald Publishing Limited
Howard House, Wagon Lane, Bingley BD16 1WA, UK

First edition 2023

Reprints and permissions service
Contact: permissions@emeraldinsight.com

British Library Cataloguing in Publication Data
A catalogue record for this book is available from the British Library

ISBN: 978-1-80455-148-6 (Print)
ISBN: 978-1-80455-147-9 (Online)
ISBN: 978-1-80455-149-3 (Epub)

ISOQAR certified
Management System,
awarded to Emerald
for adherence to
Environmental
standard
ISO 14001:2004.

Certificate Number 1985
ISO 14001

INVESTOR IN PEOPLE

To my husband, Alessio, with endless gratitude and love

Contents

About the Author

Anna Irimiás is Associate Professor of Tourism Management at the Corvinus University of Budapest, Hungary. Her research interests include consumer behaviour, tourism destination management, cultural tourism and film tourism.

Acknowledgements

This volume has come to fruition, thanks to the encouragement of many friends and colleagues. I would like to acknowledge the support of the Series Editor Richard Sharpley (University of Central Lancashire, Preston, UK) and to Sheena Reghunath (Emerald Editorial team). Writing of this book took place between June and November 2022 in Budapest for which I acknowledge the support of the Corvinus University of Budapest (Hungary). I am indebted to Gábor Michalkó and Ariel Mitev (Corvinus University of Budapest) for their critical insights and for our discussions around the kitchen table. The photos and insights from young tourists, Nicole Betta, Zsófia Fekete, Fiamma Gomes, Eszter Klapka, Edoardo Marangon and Zsófia Szabó, are particularly valuable to this volume. Thanks for sharing them. I am also grateful to Maria Della Lucia (University of Trento, Italy) who insisted that I should 'write that book'.

Finally, the support of my husband Alessio, my daughter Caterina, my parents Judit and György and my mother-in-law Sandra has been essential to the completion of this book.

Anna Irimiás
Budapest, Hungary

Introduction

I've come up with a set of rules that describe our reactions to technologies.

1. *Anything that is in the world when you're born is normal and ordinary and is just the natural part of the way the world works.*
2. *Anything that is invented between when you are fifteen and thirty-five is new and exciting and revolutionary and you can probably get a career in it.*
3. *Anything invented after you are thirty-five is against the natural order of things.*

(Douglas Adams, 1979, *Hitchhiker's Guide to the Galaxy.*)

The world is currently home to the highest number of young people in human history, and youth tourism is viewed as the fastest growing segment of international tourism (UNWTO, 2016). Getting to know young people has never been an easy task. Historically, the young were often seen by their elders as problematic, irresponsible and a cause for concern, while young people frequently complain that gerontocracy limits their ambitions, dreams and passions. These laments, and stereotypes, are still prevalent today. And there is now a huge gap between the generations in terms of information communication technology use. In general, of course, the young today are neither better nor worse than previous generations; they are just different. Discovering how different they really are is no easy task, largely because contemporary young people tend to be more open with their peers than with their parents, not to mention researchers.

Young people are widely described as 'our future'. The concept of 'future', however, is vague. The more distant it is, the more abstractly we perceive it. Arguably, positioning the young in an abstract space/time dimension alienates them from the present. Referring to the young in normative discourses as 'our future' often serves as a way to justify their non-involvement or exclusion from decision-making. Such alienation in space and time also raises some ethical issues. Very often the young – 'the/our future' – are exhorted to resolve problems created in the past and fuelled in the present. Climate change, over-consumption and overtourism are some of these issues directly related to tourism. Politicians, institutions and older generations are highly paternalistic in their dealings with the young. At the same time, as the Secretary General of the United Nations, António Guterres (2019) has pointed out that older people often insist that those who have not yet been born are going to have to solve problems and issues caused by their ancestors.

The Youth Tourist: Motives, Experiences and Travel Behaviour, 1–4
Copyright © 2023 by Anna Irimiás
Published under exclusive licence by Emerald Publishing Limited
doi:10.1108/978-1-80455-147-920231001

Normative discourses in academia on the young shape our understanding of youth tourists, seen as tech-savvy, narcissistic and in search of personalised products and services. As experts in discourse analysis have widely evidenced, there is often a – rather negative – subtext lurking beneath the language used in the media and in academia to describe young tourists, and careful analysis of it is therefore always necessary (Carvalho, 2008). Although there have been warnings about the 'sin of homogenisation' and the stereotyping of tourists (Pearce, 2011, p.18), current normative discourse on the young continues to reinforce certain stereotypes which are all too easy to fall into, especially when we are trying to quickly and easily identify a consumer segment.

In the 25 years since Neil Carr (1998) pointed out that the young were largely ignored by researchers, a plethora of studies on youth tourism – in part motivated by the increasing importance of the market segment that they represent – has explored young adults' travel motivations and behaviour. In tourism studies that adopt a market growth approach, young tourists, very often called 'millennials' without specifically mentioning an age cohort, are lumped together as consumers with similar attitudes and tourism behaviours. This approach persists, even though both academics and practitioners have long acknowledged significant differences in young tourists' social status, interests and behaviour (e.g. Khoo-Lattimore & Liang Yang, 2018; Richards, 2015). Our knowledge about young tourists is also very partial because many tourism studies use college students as their sample. Here, I draw on psychologist Jeffrey Jensen Arnett's (2016) conceptualisation of 'emerging adulthood'. According to Arnett, late adolescents and young adults should be defined as 'emerging adults' on the basis of developmental processes. Five key aspects distinguish emerging adulthood from both puberty (13–17) and fully fledged adulthood (30–45): identity exploration, instability, self-focus, feeling in-between, possibilities. These themes will be explored in this volume. Select case studies from different parts of the world will illustrate the latest research on young people, with a particular focus on young tourists. Travelling alone, having to organise daily activities, going hostelling and encountering many different people are at the core of the latter's experiences.

This volume sets out to enable a comprehensive understanding of young tourists by challenging the stereotypes about them and providing an overview of the young in different disciplines. The aim is to map out the structural factors of this heterogenous segment and thereby stimulate further discussion in the field of tourism.

While several significant attempts to explore youth tourism have been made (e.g. Cohen, 2011; Selby, 2021), they have studied specific segments such as backpackers or educational tourists. The motivations of youth tourists on study abroad programs differ from those of young festival-goers. Youth tourists on family holidays, on study or work abroad programs, on pilgrimage, at festivals, or participating in media-induced tourism events all need to be specifically identified and described. In Pearce's (2005, 2022) travel career pattern, tourists' primary motives, almost invariant across age/life-stages, are novelty, escape/relax and relationships, defined as 'core motives'. These motives are surrounded by a middle layer (self-development, involvement, self-actualisation and self-enhancement) and an outer layer (social status, nostalgia, romance etc.) which indicate less important motives. Pearce (2022) points out that it is vital to recognise that human motives change as one's travel experience increases: less-travelled young people usually rate all the motives as equally important. In contrast, experienced travellers rate higher the extrinsic motives, grouped in the middle layer, more highly. In this book, I employ the travel career pattern approach (Pearce, 2005, 2022) to study young people's travel motivations, aspirations, behaviour and experience. This sort of fine-grained analysis is necessary for two reasons: first, it will help to illustrate the rich diversity of youth tourist motivations and behaviours, a heretofore under-researched tourism segment. Second, it will significantly increase our knowledge of youth tourist travel patterns and online and offline travel behaviours, which have been dramatically influenced by the current societal changes. The book offers a nuanced understanding of youth tourist demands and their implications for the market. Last, consideration of future trends in youth tourism will be highlighted while also addressing the implications of current challenges such as climate change.

This volume is divided into four chapters, each enriched with young tourists' personal insights into their experiences. Chapter 1 considers youth populations globally and in the most important tourist source countries. The impact of current societal changes on young people's everyday lives is briefly discussed in order to provide a deeper understanding of how these changes influence their tourism behaviour. A multidisciplinary perspective is adopted to explore the social construct of 'the young' and how blurred the rites of passage between life-stages have become in the last quarter century or so. Generational labels and the ways in which the cohort theory influences research on youth tourism are also discussed.

Chapter 2 focuses on personal and identity development in the context of youth tourism, particularly study and volunteer abroad programs. Emerging adults tend to seek once-in-a-lifetime experiences. Educational, spiritual, volunteer and backpacker journeys are motivated by the desire to escape, discover and learn something new, build relationships and feel autonomous. The benefits of studying abroad are analysed with a focus on intercultural sensitivity and how this competence contributes to self-enhancement. The chapter also explores the changes in many voluntourists' principal motivations: from a wish to 'do good' to the opportunity to display one's voluntourism experiences on social media.

Chapter 3 investigates the societal changes influencing both young people's leisure activities and their tourism behaviour, while recognising that distinctions and contrasts between every day and holiday behaviours are being blurred, just as our online and offline lives are: being connected 24/7 means never being fully anywhere – whether we are – supposedly – at home or on holiday, working or playing. The chapter discusses hedonistic holiday experiences from a broad perspective, and research from the fields of tourism, marketing and sociology provides insights into young tourists' behaviour. The places of tourism experiences, like the desert of the Coachella Valley Music, are read through Foucault's lens on heterotopia, as a real place that reflects a perfected society.

Chapter 4 presents a provocative discussion on the complex relationship between young tourists and social media. The meaning of wanderlust is defined and linked to digital nomads' and 'vanlifers' experiences. Additionally, the chapter aims to advance critical thinking about youth tourism in the light of omnipresent digitalisation and ubiquitous connectivity. A young tourist's autoethnographic observation of her FOMO provides a very moving example of how young tourists experience, and reflect upon, their travels.

Intended Readership

This volume is intended as a reference text for the academic market; students are its principal targets. The Covid-19 pandemic has heavily impacted young people's lives and deprived them of their tourist role. Opening up, travelling and being ready to experience 'real life' again – these are all more than simply a 'return to normal life' (whatever that means). A better understanding of youth tourist's motivations and behaviour is valuable to young tourists themselves who are concerned about their own experiences. Policymakers developing youth-oriented initiatives at the regional, national or international level could also gain a better understanding of today's 'youth' by reading this book. Tourism, as will be discussed, is closely intertwined within the spheres of education, employment and social relations. And, in all these areas, it is time to put young people centre stage.

Chapter 1

The Youth Tourism Domain

This chapter introduces the reader to the study of youth tourism, both providing a conceptualisation of youth, and highlighting the topic's relevance. It reveals the size and growth of the global market and offers an overview of the history and current trends within youth tourism. It also offers a critical literature review on generation labels and stereotypes, shedding light on the normative discourse around 'the young' and thus also around 'the youth tourist'. Youth-oriented services – the Interrail and hostels – are addresses for the importance these have in shaping youth tourism demand.

1.1. Size and Growth of the Global Youth Population

In 2023, the world's population is forecast to reach 8 billion with more than half of all people living in seven countries (Peoples' Republic of China, India, the US, Indonesia, Pakistan, Nigeria and Brazil). Today, 16 per cent of the global population is aged between 15 and 24. According to the calculations of the organisation World Population Prospects (2019), the global youth population is expected to grow to 1.4 billion over the next 40 years. In most countries, population growth and size and age structures are changing in some unprecedented ways. Analysis of World Health Organisation (2021) data suggests that by 2030 one in six individuals globally will be aged 60 or over. Ageing populations in industrialised countries, especially in core countries within the European Union (EU), are determining the policies of the welfare state. From this perspective, the young appear on the political agendas of different countries as the demographic which will be responsible for the well-being of elders. In 2010, 18.4 per cent of the total EU population was aged between 15 and 29, and in 2021, it was only 16.3 per cent. Bulgaria has the lowest rate (14.2 per cent of the total population), while Turkey (not yet a member state) has the highest at 23.0 per cent (see more on ec.europa.eu/Eurostat). The number of young people in the EU (50 million in 2021) is predicted to decrease by 15 per cent by 2100: for every 100 people of working age, there are expected to be 57 elders.

The Youth Tourist: Motives, Experiences and Travel Behaviour, 5–24
Copyright © 2023 by Anna Irimiás
Published under exclusive licence by Emerald Publishing Limited
doi:10.1108/978-1-80455-147-920231002

Normative discourses in the media often depict the youth population as either a resource or a problem. When associated with the new and creative energy that they represent, the young are described positively, when their substance [ab]use, addiction or deviant behaviour is focused on, the connotation is other. The young are often described as the 'generation of the future': the two concepts – 'youth' and 'future' – are usually interwoven with a sense of hope and a faith that young energy will create a new future. A brief overview of population demographics reveals the limitations of defining the young simply by their date of birth. Global population distribution and disparities between life cycles in different countries appear to indicate that working-age populations will increase in countries with low-labour productivity (Mason et al., 2022). If the future is predicated on the young, it is going to manifest most vibrantly where youth populations are biggest, that is, in Central Africa, where, in 2021, over 45 per cent of the population was under 15 (Fig. 1). As mentioned, the young are often associated with creative energy. In which case, at the country level, Nigeria, with its 33 million young adults, or Mexico, with one of the world's largest youth populations, can look forward to futures shaped by creativity and innovation. However, a large youth population does not automatically correlate with social well-being. In order to compare the countries referred to above, additional data are necessary. Life expectancy at birth and the percentage of the population that is ageing are also significant indicators. For example, in Germany the average life expectancy is 81.72 years, in Mexico it is 75.32 and in Nigeria only 55.12. Perceptions of youth thus differ across cultures: a 65-year-old in Italy is considered middle-aged while a 45-year-old in Gabon is not far off old age.

Normative discourses in policy documents and reports are also interesting. Youth and women – usually considered to be minorities – are often mentioned together. Both certain United Nations (UN Sustainability Development Goals, 2022) and World Economic Forum (2021) reports provide examples of this tendency. Considering young people (and women) as groups of individuals whose rights need to be recognised, acknowledged and institutionally guaranteed offers another perspective from which to study the young. The above reports describe the achievements that have been made but also clearly testify to the many challenges that youth populations face in different parts of the world. Their access to health care, safe and nutritious food, clear water and quality education is still by no means guaranteed, and I am afraid that this will continue to be the case in the decades to come. Currently, more than 30 per cent of young people globally are without safe food and water, health care or any means to access online education. The need to address these issues is now more pressing than ever. The Sustainable Development Goals (SDGs 4 and 8) set out in the Agenda 2030 include ensuring that all young people are able to enjoy quality education and decent work and living conditions. To achieve this, real commitment and concrete action are needed. Many young people globally are involved in tourism, and far more are – to varying extents – affected by it: even the most remote parts of the world are rapidly being drawn into what is an increasingly competitive tourism environment.

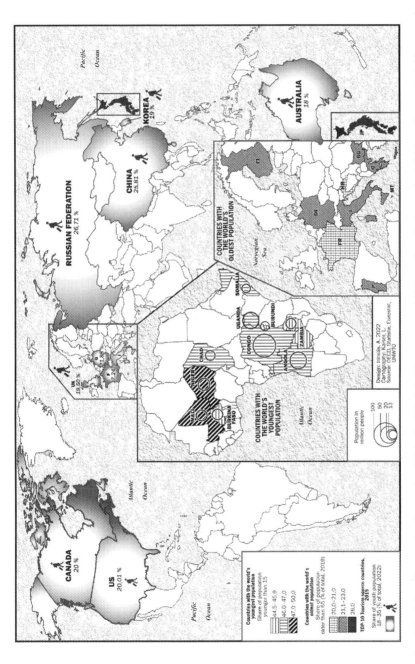

Fig. 1.   The Map Shows the Countries With the World's Youngest and Oldest Populations, the 10 Most Important (Pre-pandemic and Pre-Ukraine War) Tourism Source Countries, and the Share of the Latter's Population That Is Under 15.

1.2. Youth Populations in Tourism Source Countries

This book focuses on youth tourists. Changes in the global youth population clearly contribute to shaping the tourism market. In tourism, as in all sectors, future trends cannot be forecast without considering demographic change, and the most important tourism source countries have ageing populations (Fig. 1). Moreover, social and economic changes that affect the lives of young adults inevitably influence their travel and tourism behaviour. Starting from the strongest economy in Europe, Germany, here I provide some key figures on the demographic trends in the top three tourism source countries (People's Republic of China, the USA and Germany). These demographic trends are forecast to impact on receiving countries.

While Germany's ageing population is common knowledge, recent data on the country's population trends took many by surprise. In 2021, Germany's youth population was a lower percentage of the overall than it had ever been (Destatis, 2022). In a country of over 80 million inhabitants, 21.88 per cent were aged between 18 and 35, and only 10 per cent, 8.3 million people, were aged between 15 and 24. The US population is also getting older but is forecast to age more slowly than that of the EU. People born between 1981 and 1996, the so-called millennials, currently constitute the largest adult generation (73 million). They are more educated and earn more than previous American generations did at the same age. Hispanics are projected to become the largest ethnic minority by Pew Research Centre (2020). Turning to China, the size and spending power of its young tourists have attracted the attention of tourism service providers and academics. In 2022, the youth population in China accounted for 25.81 per cent of the total population. Currently, China's zero-Covid policy is severely restricting the country's travel market. However, before the pandemic, studies revealed Chinese millennials to be keen to pursue their passions, seeking meaningful and exciting travel experiences, an ideal tourism source market for many destinations.

1.3. 'Youth': A Concept That Needs Definition

Age, along with gender and nationality, is one of the demographic descriptors used in tourism studies. The concept of youth appears in very diverse contexts; however, research often assumes that it can be understood univocally: the young are those who belong to a certain age-cohort. Studies in sociology have indicated that it is difficult to find a consensus on what it means to be 'young'. As some research shows, the concept of youth is a social construct. The fact that social scientists, policy-makers, marketers and the media all employ different concepts of youth makes it very hard to know what we are actually defining, and there is an ever-present risk that 'stereotypes, clichés, memes, targets, scapegoats, folk devils, stigma, discourses and signifiers' enter into our descriptions (Threadgold, 2019, p.3).

The standard – Oxford English Dictionary (2022) – definition of youth is: 'the period from puberty till the attainment of full growth, between childhood and adult age'. In order to conceptualise the young, we need to reflect on childhood and adulthood and on how the lengthening transition period between the two has changed the social and cultural imagery of youth. Social scientists generally agree that the nature of adulthood has changed, and that being an adult now is not like it was five decades ago. Today's societies have been disrupted by rapid social, economic and cultural change that poses challenges for young adults, their families and society at large. The Covid-19 pandemic has given rise to new economic and employment uncertainties which make it even harder for the young to reach decisions about education, work and family.

The social imagery around adulthood has also undergone significant transformations in recent decades (du Bois-Reymond, 2015). At the beginning of the twentieth century, adolescence was a relatively brief life-stage. Few people in their 20s were still in formal education, and the passage from school graduation to marriage and parenthood was rapid. Adulthood was associated with financial autonomy and living independently. Of course, the age at which one reaches adulthood depends on place of birth and the opportunities available: adulthood and consequently youth and young adulthood are defined differently across cultures (Bird & Krüger, 2005). Being financially independent and making individual choices are associated with adulthood in Western societies. Having emotional self-control and respecting social norms are adult achievements in India. Young adults in Nordic countries usually leave home after secondary school, while many young people in southern Europe continue to live with their parents until they move in with a long-term partner.

Current social changes have compelled many young adults to stay at home longer or to return to live with their parents after a period of living independently. Emerging adulthood is a developmental period from adolescence to the late 20s, the period in which many people are most likely to explore their identity and experience instability in various guises. Chart 1 illustrates the divisions

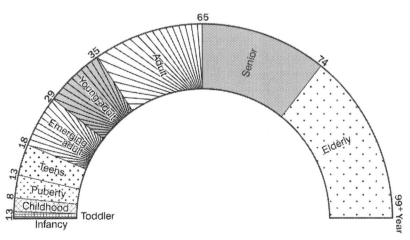

Chart 1.   The Human Lifespan and Its Age-cohorts. *Source*: Author's elaboration (2022).

of life into age-cohorts, evidencing 'emerging adulthood'. Getting off to a 'slow start' is a term used to refer to the fact that young people are spending longer in education, embarking on career paths later, postponing their assumption of responsibility, settling down and having children later (du Bois-Reymond, 2015). In sum, they are delaying their assumption of adult roles. This 'slow start' has long-term effects on society at large and will also inevitably shape trends in tourism. In 2007, Bauman (2007, p.9) observed that employers prefer 'free floating, unattached and flexible employees' with no bonds and commitments. In other words, the demands of the job market are partly responsible for these delays when transitional life-events take place and hence when fully fledged adulthood can be realised.

This consideration of societal changes and evolving concepts of youth, in the sense of period of life, allows us to take another step towards a more nuanced understanding of young tourists. Before doing so, let us briefly consider the approaches adopted within different disciplines to relate to the young and the social changes influencing their lives. Then, I will reflect in detail on the three features used to describe young tourists. The approaches and perspectives adopted to study young people today can very profitably be applied in tourism research to broaden our view and enrich our understanding of this multifaceted population. In the paragraphs below I draw on the broad interdisciplinary field of youth studies and the ontological lens of 'youth' to explore the complexity of young adult experience and how this relates to tourism from the demand side. I briefly describe how youth is conceptualised in educational research, social psychology, youth and child sociology and youth transition research.

Educational research encompasses all the subjects involved in formal and informal learning. In the pedagogical textbooks and within the education system, the young are identified as learners, and educational research emphasises the role of (formal) instruction in personal development. According to the statistics, the educational level of young populations in all industrialised countries is rising; however, almost everywhere, actual standards are dropping. At the same time, the general approach to learning has changed significantly. Across age groups, a growing number of people are engaged in life-long learning, informal learning, the acquisition of social competences and skills. Consequently, the tendency to simply equate 'learner' and 'young person' now needs to be reassessed.

Similarly, recent research in social psychology challenges the definition of youth as a mere question of age-cohort. Sociologist James Côté (2014) argues that age brackets mark life-stages and that simply playing around with where we place these brackets does little to further our understanding of the (complex) concepts of 'extended adolescence' or 'young adulthood'. Drawing on identity capital theory, Côté adapts the 'agency' approach and stresses the importance of young people developing their social capital and identity in order to reach their potential. He also warns against the risk of generalising young adults either as individuals hindered by structural obstacles or, conversely, as solely responsible for achieving their goals and optimising their potential as agents.

Youth and child sociology provide relevant insights on the social in/exclusion of young people from different cultural, social, familiar and religious backgrounds. Childhood is considered a key life-stage in developmental psychology. An interesting approach is emerging in child sociology which differs from the studies on puberty and adolescence. The restrictions imposed on children and the continuous adult supervision that they experience no longer apply when they become young adults. Nor do these same young adults have to assume the responsibilities and commitments of independent adult life. The current prolongation of young adulthood also appears to be occurring at the same time as a shortening of childhood. Many 8–9 years old behave and talk like 12-year-olds. Child sociology considers the child independently from his/her caregiver and acknowledges children's autonomy and their right to make decisions (although in practice this right is often denied, for multiple reasons). From this perspective, children are 'agents'.

Youth transition research draws on life-cycle and generation theory (Howe & Strauss, 1991). The conceptualisations of adulthood in current normative discourses have changed. 'Adulthood' is the stage to which youth transitions. Human life-stages are marked by transitions: from school to workplace, from family home to independent living, from being single to living in a relationship. In the social imagery of the Fordist era, young adults were supposed to move from school to the labour market and to 'settle down' (Bird & Krüger, 2005). Life-trajectories were pre-established with strictly imposed gender roles. The 'big five' markers of adulthood (leaving home, finishing school, permanent employment, marriage and children) were conceptualised as the life-stages through which one transitioned. The various life-cycle stages are usually marked by rites of passage. These (secular or religious) symbolic passages are present in all cultures and herald the transformation from one life-stage to another. In fact, being young is understood as living in years of 'transition' through adolescence towards adulthood (Blatterer, 2010). Fifty years ago, the 'big five' were achievable by most members of society. Today, these life-changing events are being delayed. Moreover, the labour market requires young adults to be flexible, mobile, willing to relocate and retrain and responsible for their own self-development (Blatterer, 2010). The milestones of adulthood, the opportunity to have a permanent job, own a home and live with a permanent partner seem to be out of reach for many. The longer periods that young adults are spending at home with their parents often lead to them being defined as in 'extended adolescence', even when their choices are dictated by structural factors (unemployment, student debt, etc.). Relatively important rites of passage such as coming-of-age parties and graduation ceremonies are good examples of life-stage transition markers; however, these rites do not now necessarily symbolise a genuine transition from youth to adulthood.

According to Pierre Bourdieu, youth is a social construct and should be understood as standing in opposition to old age since adulthood is 'constructed in *the struggle* between the young and the old' (Bessant et al., 2020, p.77). Any division into age-cohorts is subject to manipulation because the division between young and old is about power relations. Bourdieu (1986) discusses the importance of social, cultural and economic capital, which strengthen each other and are exchangeable. Cultural capital is formed within the family, the environment where *habitus* develops. Social capital is formed at school, and through the social interactions it is necessary to perceive oneself in relation to others. *Habitus* understood as cultural capital relates to 'agency' and refers to the idea that young people are in charge of themselves and empowered to decide their life-trajectories. Drawing on the concepts of *habitus* and cultural capital, tourism research can shed light on youth tourists' attitudes, tastes, preferences and behaviours. Being young is an in-between life-stage neither child nor yet fully adult. We are living in 'liquid modernity' (Bauman, 2000), and youth tourists' experiences also occur in spatial-temporal fluidity. Liquid modernity accords more value to transformation and immediacy than to stability and long-term commitment. Bauman warned against the consumption-focus of this liquid modernity, in which people construct their identities through their purchases, and having is more important than being. Advertisements for cosmetics, fashion and travel reinforce and promote the idea of youthfulness as a socially and culturally imperative condition. Advertising speaks to its consumers' egos and sets out to convince us that being young/youthful is a state that an ever-expanding number of age-cohorts can aspire to.

1.4. Generational Labels for the Young

Tourism research studies often refer to the concept of 'generations' to investigate the consumer behaviour of a particular segment. Cohort theory posits that key social, historical and cultural events occurring in a given time and space are likely to influence personality development (Corbisiero, et al., 2022). According to this theory, in which personality development is a key concept, a generation should be defined on the basis of the major – and thus formative – events that occurred when they were adolescents and young adults. Defining characteristic tourism behaviours in line with generations which are thus distinguished may be relevant when working with continuity theory (Atchley, 1993) which holds that people, as they age, attempt to preserve and sustain long-standing patterns of behaviour based on their past experiences, starting with, naturally, those of their youth. This theory implies that sociohistorical events in each generation's lifetime shape common generational attitudes, preferences and behaviours and that these persist as cohorts grow older. The commonly used terms millennial and generation X, Y and Z are situated within the theoretical framework of cohort theory, and the development and use of information and communication technology is seen as a key feature of the lives of these cohorts (Corbisiero et al., 2022). In the People's Republic of China, generations are defined by half-decades and decades, thus today's young are people born 'post-1995' or 'post-2000'. Young Chinese are often referred to as 'the strawberry generation' (Xie, 2022) and are perceived as reluctant to tolerate hardship. Male children born under the rigid one-child policy – officially reversed in 2016 – are called 'Little Emperors', a reflection of the fact that they are considered to have received the undivided – and excessive – attention of their parents.

The Washington-based Pew Research Centre (PRC) collects data on social, economic and demographic trends and attitudes related to issues that include politics, immigration, religion, gender, generation and age. Their working definition of a 'generation' refers to a group of people of the same age who display collective attitudes and behaviours. The PRC (2019, 2020) has found 'millennials' (born between

1981 and 1996) to be an analytically meaningful generation and has been studying it for more than a decade. Research centres such as the PRC, however, rarely explain how they choose to define a particular generation. PRC (2019) has shown that most Millennials came of age and entered the job market during the economic recession; the resulting economic and social environment influenced their life choices and career trajectories. Many had to stay at home with their parents for longer than (had become) normal.

Table 1 provides a structure within which to define the different generations alive in 2023. While generations are often defined by year of birth, the boundaries between them cannot be drawn arbitrarily. Sociohistorically based generations, rather than chronological age-cohorts, appear to provide a more useful framework within which to categorise intragenerational attitudes, behaviours and

Table 1. Western-view Definition of Generations According to Birthyear, Key Historical Events and Travel Characteristics.

Generation Name	Year of Birth	Historical Event in Childhood	Age in 2023	Characteristic Tourism Behaviours
The silent generation	1928–1945	World War II Great Depression	Between 78 and 95	Planned leisure trip for relaxation
Baby boomers	1946–1964	Post-war economic boom Great social changes	Between 59 and 77	Loyal tourists
Generation X	1965–1980	Economic stagnation	Between 43 and 58	Frequent travellers
Generation Y/Millennials	1981–1996	Fall of the Berlin Wall Tiananmen Square	Between 27 and 42	Travel more than any other previous generation
Generation Z	1997–2011	9/11 Terrorist attack War in Iraq and Afghanistan	Between 26 and 12	Frequent travellers, view travel as a priority
Generation Alpha 'Pandemials'	2012 Onwards	Covid-19 pandemic Climate change War in Ukraine	11 and under	Used to travelling with their millennial parents, have experienced lockdowns

Sources: Author's elaboration based on Pew Research Centre (PRC, 2019), Corbisiero et al. (2022) and Lehto et al. (2008).

preferences (Pearce, 2011). By acknowledging that formative experiences (e.g., in recent decades, the Covid-19 pandemic, the economic recession or the advent of social media) interact with people's life-stages, it is possible to assess the ways in which historical events shape people's world views, as reflected in their particular generation. In Table 1, the oldest generation is referred to as the 'silent generation'. Age-cohorts after 1965 are labelled with letters from the Latin alphabet (Gen X, Y and Z), while the generations born after 2011 are labelled with letters from the Greek alphabet (Table 1).

The use of birthyear as the sole determinant of a tourist segment can be misleading because, as pointed out previously, young people vary. Some research defines generations according to age-cohort and shared experience of the historical events that occurred during their transformative years. The human life-cycle, including ageing, is a developmental process influenced by multiple factors (Lehto et al., 2008). The political, economic and social events that occur in one's lifetime may significantly influence how one ages, as do access to quality education and health services, job opportunities and leisure time. Ruspini (2022) argues that the key historical events that take place during the transition between a generation's childhood and adulthood could provide a marker for that generation.

1.5. Normative Discourse on 'Youth Tourists' in Tourism Studies

The youth segment is understood as a group of people in the same age-cohort, usually 18- to 30-year-olds, defined as 'emerging adults' (Arnett, 2016). Young tourists represent an economically and socially prominent market segment, according to the United Nations World Tourism Organisation (UNWTO, 2016). This prominent market segment has recently gained the attention of both tourism stakeholders and academics.

The World Youth Student & Educational Travel Confederation (WYSE, 2019, p.7) definition of youth tourism is worthy of note. Members of this not-for-profit organisation operate in the field of youth tourism, and most are service providers, serving more than 40 million young tourists per year, in a total of 70 countries. Before the Covid-19 pandemic, about 23 per cent of international arrivals were estimated to be young tourists (WYSE, 2021). This is the Confederation definition of young tourists:

> International independent travel for periods of less than one year by people aged 15 to 29 motivated, in part or in full, by a desire to experience other cultures (including cultural exchange visits), build life experience and/or benefit from formal and informal learning opportunities outside one's usual environment.

Note that the age-cohort (15–29) coincides with Arnett's (2016) 'emerging adulthood' developmental stage.

In the WYSE's definition the emphasis is on learning opportunities and cultural exchanges, and this reflects the member organisations' profiles within the

Confederation. Richards and Morrill (2020) report on a global youth travel survey that examines the motivations (social, relaxation, intellectual and competence-mastery) and travel behaviour of young travellers under the age of 35. This data evidences the significant differences in travel motivations across world regions – Asians tend to travel more for relaxation and European, American or Australasian counterparts seek adventure – and also shows that young people travel to explore, relax and to gain new knowledge. Here, 'young tourists' are aged between 15 and 35 (Chart 2).

Narratives on young tourists are changing. A few decades ago, youth tourists were defined as money-poor and time-rich, although some research had already shown that in terms of total spending youth tourism is not confined to 'budget-tourism' (Richards & Wilson, 2005). In recent studies, youth tourists are referred to as a significant segment in the tourism market with high purchasing power (Khoo-Lattimore & Yang, 2018). This emerging youth market is particularly relevant in Western countries and parts of Asia. Young tourists are typically referred to as tech-savvy, innovation-minded and multitasking individuals. In fact, most tourism research has focused on efforts to understand their digital behaviour. Some sociologists have criticised this characterisation as overly romantic and warned against the risks of stereotyping this extremely homogeneous group of individuals based simply on their use of technology.

Social science researchers who adopt the generation lens suggest that if we see a 'generation' as a relatively homogeneous entity it is possible to gain considerable insights into the individual attitudes and behaviours of that generation's members. Millennials are one of the most frequently discussed generations (Benckendorff et al., 2010). The conceptualisation of millennials based on their (unique) characteristics and linking these generational characteristics to individual attitudes and behaviours might reasonably be expected to provide interesting insights for tourism research. While, for example, comparing generational use of apps and

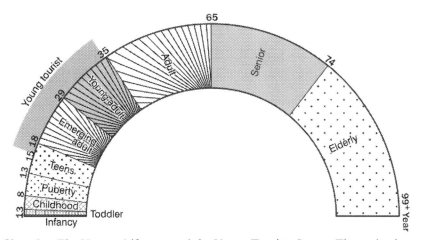

Chart 2.   The Human Lifespan and the Young Tourist. *Source*: The author's elaboration (2022).

digital devices when visiting a tourist attraction will reveal real differences, social scientists need to be aware of how heterogeneous young adults (and elders, too) are. Given the prevalence of the generational label in tourism research on youth tourists, here I provide a critical review of how these labels are used in normative discourses. Since young tourists are often categorised as millennials, that is where we will start.

1.6. Millennials

During the summer of 2022, *Corriere della Sera*, one of Italy's leading daily newspapers, posed a question: are millennials a lost generation, or ready to take their place in society? In the journalist's analysis, even though millennials have started to turn 40, they are still struggling to find recognition and to really fit in. They were born pre-smartphones, use the Internet regularly, have average salaries, conceptualise family in a new way and are able to reinvent themselves. Another trend is that entering the job market and society generally is becoming more difficult: the young are reaching adolescence earlier but adulthood later. This is in line with sociological studies that argue that the erosion of work and cultural values as sources of meaning and identity drives young adults to look for these things in the world of consumption and leisure.

Since the boundaries of the age-cohort defined as 'young' are extending, the 'youth tourist' market segment is growing and becoming more heterogenous. Most studies argue that millennials consider tourism to be a natural, taken-for-granted activity. According to Migacz and Petrick (2018, p.20), millennials should be grouped as 'young and free millennials' (YFM) and 'professional millennials' (PM) on the basis of their household income and experience of travelling. YFMs are more interested in exploration, education and novelty than PMs who travel for rest and relaxation. Cavagnaro et al. (2018) investigated the tourism experiences of 423 Dutch Millennials by analysing their value orientation and the meaning they give to travel. Ten value orientations (security, power, achievement, hedonism, stimulation, self-direction, benevolence, tradition, conformity and universalism) and four travel meanings (inner development, interpersonal exchange, socialising and entertainment, escapism and relaxation) were identified. The young tourists described in the four micro-trends are highly privileged and represent only a small segment of the global youth population. The reality for many – and not only the most excluded – is very different: a compound of unstable, poorly paid, and alienating work, joyless leisure, stunted social and personal relationships. Results show that notwithstanding all the shared characteristics that distinguish millennials from previous generations, they are not a homogeneous tourist group. Ketter (2021) applied content analysis to academic articles and trend reports and argued that 'European Millennials' rank travel as a top priority and perform all travel stages on their smartphones. By analysing tourist characteristics and travel behaviours, he outlined four micro-trends: (1) the increasing popularity of creative tourism; (2) a preference for off-the-beaten track tourism; (3) a preference for alternative forms of accommodation; and (4) the ubiquity of digitalisation and ICT services in tourism.

Millennials thus seem to be 'fully digital' open-minded travellers who tend to avoid traditional tourism services.

Building on cohort theory, Corbisiero et al. (2022, p.24) studied tourism with a focus on millennials and the future of tourism. They argue that 'generations take shape within a specific sociohistorical location' and the social circumstances and epochal events that they experience (together) crucially determine their worldviews, values, attitudes and behaviours. Millennials are often referred to as the tech-savvy generation: they – and their lives – have been profoundly shaped by digital technologies and social media. Digitalisation is ubiquitous in young people's lives and the young are accustomed to using apps to pay in shops and bars, to rent electric scooters, to book train tickets, in other words, whenever they are required to use money. Recently, implantable payment microchips in the hand have become popular payment methods. The microchips are injected under the skin and permit rapid and easy contactless payment. This development is part of the push towards a human/tech interface in which technology gets ever closer to human body, first smartphones that are experienced by their users as extensions of their own bodies (Dwivedi et al., 2022), then smartwatches that monitor our movements and body functions, now the technology has actually been integrated into its human 'companion'. A great deal of research has been done on how young tourists integrate and use technological devices, virtual and augmented reality, and digital communication platforms (e.g., Buhalis & Sinarta, 2019; Magasic & Gretzel, 2020; Volo & Irimiás, 2022). Youth tourism studies are currently prioritising the search for ways to personalise tourism offerings, to engage users and to better understand youth tourists' preferences, tastes and behaviour through the use of digital technologies.

Some tourism studies have generalised about millennials and assumed young people's lifestyles, attitudes and behaviours to be similar all over the world. For example, Pop et al. (2022, p.11) investigating young people's attitudes to adventure tourism, claimed that

> a peculiarity of *the millennials is to have about the same habits all over the world,* due to the progress of technology and the way in which it communicates and interacts from a social point of view.

This viewpoint minimises cultural differences and reflects Pop et al.'s (2022) ethnocentric approach.

From a travel and tourism perspective, young people's attitudes, values and preferences should be a critical concern for the travel industry, whether dealing with the Global North or the South. Sensitivity to the characteristics of Millennials, Generation Z and the youngest – 'Alpha' – generation could translate into competitive advantage for destination marketers (Table 2). This volume focuses on youth tourists who are unlikely to display the same values, preferences, attitudes and behaviours in tourism and travel. Most Millennials are in adulthood, many are parents: young adults in their 20s belong to another generation, called 'Pandemials'.

Table 2. Some Young Tourists' Characteristics Mentioned in Selected Tourism Studies.

Dimensions	Youth Characteristics	Academic Resource
Technology	Digital natives, tech-savvy, always connected, technologically wired Information technology literate Able to multitask Use of sharing economy platforms Short attention spans	Benckendorff et al. (2010) Ketter (2021) Skinner et al. (2018) Bernardi (2018)
Personality	Concerned about sustainability Open to change Well-educated Optimistic, responsible, innovation-minded Sceptical, narcissistic, bored	Lewis et al. (2021) Richards and Morrill (2020) Tan and Yang (2021)
Sociality	Positive views on diversity and social issues, strong orientation towards family and social groups Politically engaged, more progressive than their predecessors, accepting of plural family settings Closely interconnected with friends and families Less trusting of institutions (government, church, etc.)	Cavagnaro et al. (2018) Selby (2021) Pop et al. (2022)
Work, employment	Preferring collaboration to competition Looking for more in life than 'just a job' Flexible working hours and importance of work-life balance are more important than financial rewards High purchasing power	Williams and Page (2011) Richards (2015) Migacz and Petrick (2018)

Source: Author's elaboration.

1.7. Youth and the Pandemic – Pandemials

Pandemials are the children and adolescents who have lost two years of school and formal education during the Covid-19 pandemic. Academic research foresees that this educational gap is likely to translate into fewer opportunities for future economic and social participation for many. During the Covid-19 pandemic, the world seemed to forget about the young. The meaning of time is recognised as an important question in tourism behaviour studies (Pearce, 2011). Children, teenagers, young adults and millennials perceive time and its passing in different ways. Two years of pandemic may be perceived as the 'end of the world' by teens and people in their 20s. Indeed, many young people consider the two years between early 2020 and early/mid-2022 to have been lost to the pandemic. During informal conversations, some young adults have told me that they feel like 23 years old, even though they are 25 according to their birthyear. Travelling alone and/or abroad is often considered a 'turning point' or life-altering experience for young adults and the ability to shape these experiences and give them meaning has been related to young adults' psychological and physical well-being. The current mental health epidemic among children and young adults is a serious issue which has not received enough attention from policy-makers or adults in general.

Emerging adults today are particularly vulnerable due to rapidly changing job market conditions, short-term contracts – especially in the service industries like tourism and hospitality – and the resultant career instability which makes it harder to reliably access social welfare benefits and reskilling opportunities. Moreover, in the United States, many young people are economically crippled by record levels of student debt. There is a growing sense globally that the generation in power has betrayed the young, as demonstrated by numerous youth protests. Inefficient policies on social and climate justice, a lack of political change and high corruption levels have all led to a youth population that is disillusioned with public and private institutions. The Covid-19 pandemic has exacerbated this mood since young people were so obviously nowhere near the top of any country's political agenda.

The impact of the Covid-19 pandemic on contemporary youth tourism cannot be minimised. Prior to the pandemic, a significant number of Western students took a gap year to experience new places, learn about different cultures and people and build social relations. During the pandemic, Generations Z and Alpha could only stay connected with other people in virtual worlds (Richards & Morrill, 2020). Post-pandemic, the youth travel market has been one of the fastest growing travel markets. Covid-19 presented the tourism sector with a major and evolving challenge and undermined the democratisation of travel, making international travel a more upmarket product, available only to the wealthier. The pandemic, inflation, climate change: all issues that are changing discourses about 'the right to travel' and whether travel should be subsidised for those unable to afford it.

In October 2022, a Web of Science search for the keywords 'youth' and 'tourism' in articles and book chapters in the fields of hospitality, leisure, tourism and sport resulted in 545 findings. Keywords 'millennials' and 'tourism' had 213 results, and 'Generation Y' and 'tourism' had 156 results. In consumer behaviour and service management studies, young people are often defined according to the above characteristics; however, although relevant, they only provide a very superficial understanding of youth populations. The Web of Science results clearly show the interest in young tourists and the diverse labels we use to describe them (Table 2).

1.8. Generation Alpha – Children and Preschoolers

Most academic studies investigate young people's tourism and consumption behaviours in isolation, but the young are, of course, part of society. Nevertheless, some general assumptions about youth tourists tend to persist in tourism behaviour research. The first is that children belong to a homogeneous group. The second is that they are all equipped with the latest technology and devices. According to a report (McCrindle, 2020), Generation Alpha – currently primary school students, children of millennial parents – has access to more information and technology than any other generation before them. Gen Alpha is often referred to as the multitasking generation; it also seems to spend a significant part of its life gazing at a screen and to be the generation with the shortest attention span and poorly developed social skills. During adolescence, moods, emotions and feelings fluctuate more than in adulthood and (offline and online) social networks impact young people's behaviour significantly. Indeed, children's participation in tourism-related decision-making makes them important agents (Canosa & Graham, 2022). In many markets (food, toys, fashion, etc.), young people have a strong voice in deciding what to buy with their own money or influencing adults in their purchases. Children and young adults' tastes and preferences drive market trends both in countries with few babies like Italy, Japan and the People's Republic of China, and in countries with high birth rates like India and the USA (Le Bigot et al., 2007).

In recent decades, social networks which began by connecting people who knew each other in 'real life' have become platforms for connections and interactions that take place solely in a digital and mediatised space. Social media networks and the human interactions in cyberspace that they permit have freed personal networks from the constraints of geography and physical space. Social media employ web-based technologies to create highly interactive platforms on which users view, create and share content. Very young children are going online and doing so in more diverse ways; social networking is one of their most common activities. Online and video gaming increased in popularity during the lockdowns and relieved feelings of isolation. However, studies show that children and young people have struggled to establish social relations with their peers even when they had previously been connected to them on the same online platforms (Webster et al., 2021). Adults' attitudes and their impact on how children are socialised must also be taken into account. Alpha-children (born in the New Millennium) have seen their parents glued to their smartphones instead of talking to each other, playing games online rather than out in the garden or at the park, communicating on Messenger, WeChat or WhatsApp rather than looking into the eyes of their interlocutor. The impact of these behavioural models is yet to be assessed, but paediatricians have already noted the deteriorating mental health of some children.

1.9. Youth-oriented Policies Within the EU

Travelling appears to be a common aspiration for young Europeans. After two years of the Covid-19 pandemic when travelling was restricted, 2022 was declared by the EU the 'European Year of Youth'. The EU Commission provided various opportunities to go abroad for work or study, whether as a volunteer, as a trainee or on a school or youth exchange (https://europa.eu/youth/home_en).

   In 2018, the EU launched the DiscoverEU initiative in collaboration with the Erasmus+ Programme (https://europa.eu/youth/discovereu_it). Under this initiative, 18-year-old European residents can apply for a free travel pass and wander around Europe for a month. In 2022, 19- and 20-year-olds could also apply since the scheme had been paused during the Covid-19 pandemic. The Erasmus programme, one of the EU's flagship projects, supports youth study abroad, education and sport both in Europe and the countries within the Erasmus+ Programme. The latter is intended to stimulate social inclusion and to promote youth participation in democratic life. Erasmus+ has an estimated budget of €26.2 billion for the period 2021–2027, almost double that of the previous period (2014–2020). More than 130,000 young people have been awarded a travel pass since the programme began.

> DiscoverEU enables you, as a young person, to develop life skills of value to your future, such as independence, confidence, and openness to other cultures.

   The EU Commission's decision to designate 2022 the 'European Year of Youth' was a significant public policy step. It is now more than ever in the interest of tourism marketers and service providers to better understand just who these young tourists are, how they make their travel decisions and how they behave when on holiday. In 2022, the first Global Youth Tourism Summit was launched with the aim of drawing children and young adults into discussions about responsible and sustainable tourism. The initiative brought together UN officials, decision-makers, industry stakeholders, celebrities and young people from many different parts of the world (https://gyts.org/about).

1.10. Interrail – The Sustainable Way to Travel

Interrail – a single cross-national rail travel pass – dates back to 1972 and thus celebrated its 50th birthday in 2022. Giving young EU citizens the opportunity to travel and discover the countries and cultures of their continent is a powerful tool for strengthening their sense of European citizenship, and the DiscoverEU programme therefore provides a very valuable resource. According to DiscoverEU data, 350,000 candidates applied for the available travel passes in 2018–2019. Two-thirds of the candidates were travelling for the first time out of their home country by train, and it was the first time that many of them had travelled without their parents or any accompanying adults. When launched in 1972, Interrail was much appreciated by parents who considered travelling by train safer than hitch-hiking (Manka, 2022). Even though the Iron Curtain still divided Europe, the Interrail services crossed the borders of some Socialist countries (Hungary, Yugoslavia and Romania), enabling young Western Europeans to get to know and establish bonds with Eastern Europeans. In the 1970s, Interrail was highly popular among young Scandinavians of all social backgrounds. The scheme's popularity peaked in 1990 and then rapidly declined. Manka (2022), through interviews and photo elicitation, explored the development of a sense of belonging to Europe and to their home country for Finnish Interrail travellers between 1972 and 1991. The author analysed the month-long Interrail journeys using written narratives accessed on social media and, interestingly, accounts collected by the Finnish Literature Society. National symbols, like the Finnish flag on people's backpacks, were considered signifiers and helped youth travellers to create a community, stimulating their sense of belonging. However, Trandberg Jensen et al. (2016), in their study on staging Interrail mobilities, demonstrated that marketing communication discourses around free, easy and independent travel across Europe are often called into question by European rail's multiple operational management systems and nationally regulated technologies. Endeavouring to address the needs of youth travellers, Interrail has subsequently developed collaborations with accommodation services like Airbnb heritage tour (https://linktr.ee/interraileu) and Hostelworld.com and boardgames like Ticket to Ride and Soundtrack.fm to increase the appeal of train travel.

1.11. Youth-oriented Services: Hostels

Hostels are low-cost, short-term accommodation services, where tourists can book double rooms or a bed in a shared room with four or more beds, up to 12. These accommodation services offer young tourists inexpensive accommodation, proximity to the main attractions and the chance to meet like-minded people. Before the Covid-19 pandemic, Asia had the highest number of hostels (5,829), followed by Europe (4,738) and South America (2,434) (Statista, 2019). A distinguishing feature of youth travel is the importance that the young accord to socialising, with both fellow tourists and locals (Martins & Costa, 2022). Richards and Morrill (2020) explored the effects of Covid-19 on the youth travel sector and their analysis of 2,780 responses from youth travel businesses showed that the youth market has been heavily impacted. Pandemic restrictions forced youth travel accommodation structures [budget hotels and hostels – some with (4–12 bed) dormitories] to revise their offers and redesign common areas. Interestingly, most youth travel businesses have both modified their cancellation policies and increased their marketing efforts, building new partnerships to develop novel products and services.

It has been observed that 'despite their importance, popularity, and the dramatic ways they [hostels] have changed since they were first established, studies on youth hostels have been largely absent from tourism literature' (Nagy, 2016, p.272). The first youth hostels, established in Germany before the World War I, offered simple accommodation to school-age children sent to stay in them so that they could experience the countryside in an intimate atmosphere (Nagy, 2016). After World War II, more hostels were built and their roles diversified. Hostel owners, called 'hostel parents', provided entertainment and education for their guests until the mid-1980s. Today, hostels in Germany and elsewhere are professional hospitality services most of which seem to have lost their original charm. Similarly, in the UK a charity called the International Youth Hostel Federation – now Hostelling International (HI) – was founded in 1932. HI has become one of the largest hostel networks in the world, with 62 member associations operating over 3,000 hostels globally (www.hihostels.com). Gardiner et al. (2013), analysing the travel behaviour of 4,633 international students studying in Australia, found that their preferred accommodation was in order: backpacker hostels, holiday apartments, hotels/motels and camping. Being frightened of sleeping in a shared room with strangers is one of the reasons why young tourists prefer to travel in groups, with friends or fellow students. The authors found that Chinese students preferred travelling with their co-nationals, whereas Europeans and North Americans were much more likely to travel with other international students. The communal use of social spaces (kitchen, recreation rooms, laundry facilities, etc.) make hostels popular among youth tourists. In fact, as HI declares, hostels, with their shared facilities and responsible resource use, are among the earliest examples of sustainable tourism. A growing number of hostels offer additional services, such as restaurants or common rooms with billiard and co-working spaces, pools and saunas, bike rooms with washing and repair stations and ski rooms (www.youthhostel.ch). As Hajibaba and Dolnicar (2017) have pointed out, Airbnb seems to be undermining the appeal of hostels and other low-end accommodation services. Young tourists tend to choose the former when travelling in groups or staying for longer periods of time.

Budapest Maverick Urban Lodge: The Maverick hostel opened in 2007 and offers hybrid accommodation services (hotel rooms and four- to six-bed dormitories). Budapest hostels have more than 4,000 dormitory beds, and the Maverick group – which owns three hotels – is one of the city's most popular hostels, is part of the Europe Famous Hostels (https://www.famoushostels.com/) network and has also received several service quality awards. The hostel has been carefully designed and decorated, with local manufacturers and craftsmen supplying the unique furniture. Mr Molnar explained that he chose to showcase Hungarian design objects in the lobby because he feels that 'it is heart-warming for us'. The hostel's interior design and excellent urban location are its unique selling points. 'Every good party starts in the kitchen' said Mr Molnar to underline the importance of a fully equipped kitchen and the elegant common areas in the hostel. Like most newly built European hostels, Maverick has a rooftop with a bar and the spacious lobby provides separate spaces for co-working and is designed to host digital nomads. The concept of a hostel has completely changed in the last few decades. They have become more like 'lifestyle budget hotels' where social relations and a sense of belonging to a community are prioritised. As Mr Molnar pointed out, no particularly unpleasant incidents have ever occurred in his hostel, and the management ensures that its young guests behave appropriately. The year 2022 was the post-pandemic recovery, the hostel had an occupancy rate over 90 per cent from August to September, evidence of young adults' pent up travel craving (Mitev & Irimiás, 2021). Before the pandemic, youth tourists used to book their dormitory bed about two weeks before their planned arrival – now, many book a bed two days or even two hours before turning up. A vivid illustration of just how flexible and mobile youth tourists have become. Evidently, they are sometimes leaving decisions about where to travel and where to stay to the very last minute. Mr Molnar mentioned that 'travelling by train is in its Renaissance', most of his guests arrive by train. They are seeking personalised and out-of-the-ordinary tourism experiences such as caving under the Buda hills, escape rooms or parties on a cruise boat. Women-only dormitories are popular among Muslim and Asian female travellers (Personal interview with the general manager of Budapest Maverick Urban Lodge, 2022).

1.12. Conclusion

Young tourists constitute an important tourism market segment. Demographic trends all over the world, like the decreasing share of young people in the most industrialised countries and the rapid social changes that are impacting emerging adults' everyday lives impact tourism motivations and behaviour. Systematic advances in youth tourism studies have been enriched by research in sociology and psychology. While the study of youth tourism is still relatively novel – and originally it was almost entirely associated with student-tourism – the research field has expanded and matured over the last few decades. Trends in youth tourism are usually studied from a generational and cohort theory perspective. By subjecting our ideas about 'the young' to a fine-grained analysis and integrating this with the conceptualisation of youth tourism, it is possible to show what clearly distinguishes youth tourism from other tourist segments. This is the aim of the chapters that follow.

Chapter 2

The Young Tourist and Personal Development

Building on identity theory, this chapter will discuss young tourists' motivations and experiences related to study abroad, religious, working holidays, volunteerism, and backpacking tourism. In endeavouring to understand young tourists' behaviour, personal development is an area of particular interest, and Pearce (2022) includes a desire to learn and seeking a sense of fulfilment in his travel career pattern. Mobility, specifically student mobility, is an opportunity for personal growth, development and identity formation. Any consideration of young tourists' behaviour also needs to take their experiences of contrasts between freedom and constraint into account. For this reason, we look carefully at gap years and backpackers' experiences.

2.1. Identity Formation and Tourism

Youth is, of course, the period in all our lives when we develop most, both physically and – in general – psychologically. The concept of 'identity' is ubiquitous in social science. Identities are primarily forged during the years of young adulthood and people's self-view plays a critical role in their lives. Studies in social psychology (Stryker & Burke, 2000) which investigate the ways in which social structures influence notions of the self and how these ideas affect social behaviour are also highly relevant for tourism research, particularly if we assume that self-actualisation, self-gratification and the construction of self-image are very likely to be among (young) tourists' main rewards (Pearce, 2022).

Identity is a social construct shaped by many significant encounters and its formation is a long process. The behaviour through which we express our identity/ies is influenced both by external social structures and the interactions between our identity/ies and our internal (cognitive) processes. Stryker and Burke (2000, p. 288) posit that a person's identity affects their behaviour when making plans to act and argue that behaviour is a 'function of the relationship between what a person perceives in the situation and the self-meanings held by the individual'.

The Youth Tourist: Motives, Experiences and Travel Behaviour, 25–44
Copyright © 2023 by Anna Irimiás
Published under exclusive licence by Emerald Publishing Limited
doi:10.1108/978-1-80455-147-920231003

Accordingly, a person's behaviour can alter their situations. However, if identity is multifaceted and human beings possess a different identity for each social context in which they find themselves, what is the mechanism by which these identities affect their behaviour? The answer, for Stryker and Burke (2000, p. 288), lies in the concept of 'self-verification'. Self-verification is based on the extent to which an individual acts consistently with their role identity and with the way in which they want others to view them. Mismatches or discrepancies can occur between someone's actual behaviour in a situation and their identity standard, a not unknown phenomenon in tourism encounters.

Tourism, which provides opportunities for social interaction and self-exploration, can play an important role in identity formation. As Graburn (1983, p. 13) observed, 'tourism is commonly associated with major life changes, such as the emergence into adulthood'. According to Johnson et al. (2011), identity exploration and development extend beyond adolescence. Awareness of the theories around identity contributes to our understanding of young tourists' attitudes and behaviours because these theories will often shed light on the roles that tourists perform in different situations. Urry's (1994, p. 235) assumption that 'identity is formed through consumption and play' is an important starting point for understanding identity in the tourism domain. An individual's 'identity' is commonly associated with their personal characteristics, leveraged in the psychographic segmentation of tourists (Carvalho et al., 2022). In contemporary tourism literature, 'identity' has different usages, and it can refer to the culture of a people, to common identification with a group or social category or to the multifaceted-self (Adams, 2016). Travel facilitates personal transformation because extended periods spent abroad may help young people to develop in a personally meaningful way (Pearce, 2022; Ritchie et al., 2003). In the next section, education tourism experiences are discussed.

2.2. Learning and Personal Development

Learning and travel have been closely linked for centuries. In a conceptual paper, Falk et al. (2012, p. 922) argue that 'travel may foster the development of skills, knowledge and wisdom' even in situations where a tourist's main travel motivation is not explicitly educational. In other words, tourists engaged in different activities – for example, bird watching, visiting museums/national parks, sightseeing, etc. – may, it is hoped, come away with more nuanced understandings of the places and cultures with which they have been interacting (above and beyond the specific focus of their trip/journey). In this section, we examine student travel experiences as turning points in individuals' personal development. Post-secondary students constitute one of the most significant single segments of the tourism market with an increasing demand which is forecast to grow in the coming years. In the 1970s, about 1 million students travelled with student/work abroad programmes in any one year, by 2019 over 6 million did (OECD, 2021). In 2019, the USA, the UK, Canada, Australia and France were the top destinations for international students (OECD, 2021; Statista, 2022). Sixty-seven per cent of all international students in the OECD area come from developing countries. Australia has the largest share as a proportion of the total college student population, and in Luxemburg 87.2 per cent of PhD students come from abroad. Being able to get a short-term student or long-term work abroad visa is a prerequisite for any such travel. Recent changes in some EU member states and the UK's much talked about departure from the European Union (Brexit), resulting in new visa regulations, have affected aspiring students, higher education institutions, academic staff, and student recruitment agencies (Selby, 2021). The negative consequences of Brexit include the higher fees faced by students from EU countries who want to study in the UK and the fact that students with UK residence are not eligible for European study programmes (e.g. Erasmus projects). To make matters worse, the UK decided not to take part in the new (2021–2027) programme as a Program Country (https:// erasmus-plus.ec.europa.eu/the-uk-and-erasmus). These decisions will inevitably impact youth tourism between the UK and the EU.

The extent to which studying abroad fosters personal development has been recognised since the days of the Grand Tour (seventeenth century into the early twentieth) when young British, French and German aristocrats travelled around Europe to learn more about different cultures, build social relationships and just have fun (Pearce, 2022). Today, several study abroad programmes are available ranging from experiences that involve spending a couple of weeks (thesis field research, language or cooking courses) to a year abroad ((visiting) scholarships, internships). According to the UNWTO Global Report on The Power of Youth Travel (2016) 'language travel' has become particularly important: in the last decade more than 2 million students travelled abroad (mainly) to improve their language skills. Summer and Easter holiday language courses, offered by both private and public institutions, are highly popular with youth tourists. These courses vary in intensity and length – from a couple of weeks to a few months – and are available in several popular tourism destinations (Richards & Wilson, 2005). Malta has become a favourite destination for young people eager to spend time in the Mediterranean while improving their English. Spanish language courses offered in Andalucía (Spain) usually include visits to cultural sites and flamenco, salsa or merengue courses. Carvalho et al. (2022) employed cluster analysis with a sample of 1,014 language tourists to define the main segments based on language-related attitudes, motivations, behaviour and travel outcomes. Their results show that language tourists are very diverse in their levels of motivation, and the authors classify them as enthusiasts, devoted, pragmatists and the less-committed to learning.

Drawing on social influence theory, Lejealle et al. (2021) explored educational travel by investigating how students evaluate destinations and institutions when considering studying overseas. Findings show that the tourism-appeal of destinations is crucial to their decision-making process. The social influence of friends, family and social media communities is more significant than that of institutions. Study, of course, is rarely the sole motivation for participating in study abroad programmes. Stone and Petrick (2013) showed the extent to which educational tourists also engage in other activities such as sightseeing and shopping. The following description, in a young tourist's own words, gives us an insight into her experience of shopping abroad (Image 1).

Image 1.   Travel for Shopping – Bicester Village.
Shopping? – Hmm, yes, it's okay. But shopping abroad with the greatest services and experiences and the kindest shop assistants? – Anytime!! Getting to Bicester Village from London is a lovely journey. The railway guides are waiting for the passengers dressed up in Bicester Village uniform, upon arrival they offered their own branded coffee and water, the vibes in the village were so special, everyone was nice and it's truly worth a visit. On the way back to London I got to know other young people that I'm sure not gonna see again, but something connected us that day, we were sitting on the train's floor, laughing as we had so many goods with us. Since then I returned to the village like 4–5 times. (*Source*: courtesy by Eszter Klapka)

International students' experiences are transformative on different levels: knowledge acquisition, skill enhancement and identity formation (Falk et al., 2012; Michalkó, 2022; Stone & Petrick, 2013). Communication and language skills are fostered through experiences gained in multilingual and multicultural environments (Ritchie et al., 2003). The development of reflexive traits, such as self-awareness and self-confidence, is also a benefit that young adults who have participated in study abroad programmes often recall (Reisinger & Turner, 2011). Independence and adaptability are reinforced through self-discovery in out-of-school contexts and when difficulties and challenges in unfamiliar situations need to be overcome (Shaftel et al., 2007). Study abroad programmes can enhance young adults' academic achievement. The skills/competences gained and/or developed are considered important elements of an individual's identity as a responsible citizen and, in relation to our discussion in the previous chapter, a responsible adult.

In Europe, the Erasmus (**Eu**R**o**pean Community **A**ction **S**cheme for the **M**obility of **U**niversity **S**tudents) mobility programme was launched in 1987 by the European Commission to support education, youth and sport. The EU's flagship programme has enabled more than 3.5 million students to study in a foreign country for anything from three to 12 months (ec.europa.eu). Erasmus, like other study abroad programmes, aims to increase students' cultural and social capital and give them the perfect opportunity to immerse themselves in another cultural environment and to learn how to understand and appreciate cultural differences (Irimiás et al., 2020). Such experiences can greatly influence identity formation. Studying in a foreign country exposes young adults to a wide range of unfamiliar situations that need to be understood and lived through. The need to communicate with people from a different cultural background incentivises attempts to understand different views and approaches. As we all know, it can be difficult enough to reach a consensus with family members or with neighbours, let alone with people whose customs and cultural expectations may be different from ours. The wish (and the need) to understand each other implies active listening, reflection and action. These encounters become significant when they challenge our taken-for-granted beliefs and assumptions and force us to engage with habits, attitudes and behaviours that differ from, and sometimes even contradict, our own. Ideas about the self are forged through such conversations/confrontations – who am I? what do I *really* think/feel about this issue? am I wrong? In the following sections three different tourism encounters are presented: interactions with culturally different individuals; interactions with culturally similar individuals; interactions with older people.

2.3. Interactions With Culturally Different Individuals: Intercultural Sensitivity

Intercultural sensitivity is defined as an individual's perceptions and reactions to cultural differences and the ability to adapt one's attitude and behaviour to these differences and to new situations (Jackson, 2015). Young tourists in education programmes are believed to be open to multiculturality, and it is widely accepted that people who can communicate in a foreign language and have travelled and thus been exposed to other cultures during their most formative years almost automatically develop intercultural sensitivity. As we will see, however, this may not always be the case: not all students are, in fact, open to diversity or want to interrogate – or change – their own worldviews. The conceptualisations of ethnocentric and ethnorelative developmental stages have been employed as theoretical starting points in a range of tourism-related research (Kirillova et al., 2015; Reisinger & Turner, 1998).

Ethnocentrism is the belief that your culture and worldview are superior to others and the denial of the validity of different cultural values (Bennett, 1986; Hammer, 2013). The first three stages (denial, defence and minimisation) in Bennett's Developmental Model of Intercultural Sensitivity are grounded in ethnocentrism. According to Triandis (2006), all human beings are ethnocentric because we believe that what is 'normal' to us is normal to everyone, everywhere. People at the ethnocentric stage of intercultural (in)sensitivity perceive world-views other than their own as 'abnormal'. Encounters perceived as threatening are usually avoided. At this stage, an individual's ethnocentric worldview is considered superior to other worldviews and no value is perceived in cultural differences. Openness to diversity is also a prerequisite for any stand against discrimination and xenophobia. It is assumed that tourism encounters with unfamiliar cultures tend to weaken prejudices and stereotypes and study abroad programmes can consolidate long-term behavioural and attitudinal changes in young adults (Rexeisen et al., 2008). Irimiás et al. (2020) investigated how tourism students can overcome stereotypes and prejudices through learning and be stimulated to greater openness towards different cultures. However, the authors show that the process is by no means linear and automatic, and that stereotypes are only overcome when someone reflects upon their tourism experiences. Tourists at the third (minimisation) stage of intercultural sensitivity are less judgemental than those who deny or fear cultural diversity although this growing acceptance tends to be the result of a minimising of cultural differences, and the assumption that 'after all, we are all the same'. This approach can lead to the trivialisation of cultural differences and a failure to recognise them (Kirillova et al., 2015).

Ethnorelativism refers to the recognition that one's culture has to be perceived in the context of other cultures (Bennett's ethnorelative stages are: acceptance, adaptation and integration). Understanding that one's worldview is a cultural construct is the first step towards intercultural sensibility and the acceptance of cultural differences. Accepting and adapting to cultural difference allows fuller understanding of other people's behaviour. As Irimiás and Franch (2019) have argued, intercultural sensitivity can be trained and developed. Like other learning processes, developing intercultural sensitivity requires time, willingness and cognitive effort – simply being physically located in another country is not enough. So, study abroad programmes and exchanges benefit young tourists when they reflect and elaborate on their experiences and are willing to translate their gained experience into attitudinal and behavioural change (Olson & Kroeger, 2001). On the other hand, while travelling/living abroad inevitably exposes individuals to people with diverse cultural backgrounds, such challenges to one's worldview may not always produce positive change: sometimes these encounters actually reinforce ethnocentric perspectives. Divergence theory posits that since value systems and beliefs are rooted in history, individuals as social agents are resistant to changing their worldview which leads to the latter's persistence across generations (de Mooji, 2019).

Although distinguishing the different stages of intercultural sensitivity is helpful, they inevitably overlap to some extent. Intercultural sensitivity is an emotional ability, susceptible to changes of circumstance. A person may be receptive in certain (new) cultural contexts but not in others. Contemporary societies are witnessing global flows of people: study, work, love, family and friendship, leisure travel and tourism, seeking asylum – there are myriad reasons for these relocations. Convergence theory posits that these global flows and the ubiquity of new technologies and digital devices are facilitating the spread of ideas, tastes in fashion, brands and entertainment, leading to an intersection of cultures and ever more homogeneity (Irimiás et al., 2020). Questioning one's own worldview, doubting one's assumptions, really trying to listen actively and understand other people's perspectives and beliefs is not easy. In most industrialised countries children and adolescents attend multicultural schools, and it is assumed that they are accustomed to recognising the existence of a wide range of ideas and beliefs (Ritchie et al., 2003). Nevertheless, when travelling/living abroad the need to challenge what may previously have been seen as 'universal' views is very likely to be experienced more acutely than it is at home. Reflective individuals are usually able to interact with people with different views and cultural backgrounds. The enhanced soft skill of intercultural sensitivity developed through such encounters and interactions can be nurtured through further studies and travel that stimulate cultural self-awareness.

Kock et al. (2019) have applied the ethnocentric concept in tourism in a novel and thought-provoking fashion, arguing that ethnocentric tourists' main purpose in choosing domestic holidays is to support the domestic economy. From this perspective, ethnocentric tourism is a positive ingroup bias expressed in tourists' selection of national products, services and destinations. According to this (US) study, ethnocentric tourism is a home-country bias, and such ethnocentric tourist behaviour is in line with the increasing intensity and expression of patriotic feeling in the USA. In this context, domestic tourism becomes a moral obligation to support your country and your fellow Americans employed in hospitality and tourism. In the light of this increase in US tourists' patriotic motivation, the authors have revised their understanding of how tourism destination choices are made. A strong commitment to the idea of holidaying in their home country suggests that the priority is not any particular destination, its uniqueness or the quality of its offer and services, but simply the fact that these are 'American'.

As we have already seen, youth mobility to study or work abroad has been increasing in recent decades. Youth trips are also motivated by a wish or need to reconnect. Socialising is a key element of youth tourism, particularly in the aftermath of the pandemic during which young people were deprived of their tourist role (Irimiás & Mitev, 2021). In April 2022, YouGov, a global market research and data analytics company, surveyed 25,918 young adults across 25 countries about their travel attitudes and behaviour. Fifty-two per cent said that they were planning to visit friends, making it one of the top tourism motivations for that age-cohort. Visiting friends and visiting relatives, as distinguished segments (Backer et al., 2017), are also linked to study abroad programmes. Young tourists on study exchange programmes often rent accommodation in their destination city and, once they have settled in, invite friends and family members to stay. Hosting close friends or family may often be a significant experience for young tourists. Playing the role of the host comes with responsibilities and being able to show friends and relatives around a new place can enhance young tourists' self-efficacy (Pearce, 2022). Moreover, young tourists can thus strengthen their social bonds with significant others and welcome them into their new lives. Petry et al. (2022) used mixed methods to explore the different roles students played as hosts.

Their results showed that only in very rare cases did students perceive friends or relatives as just using them as somewhere to stay for free. In Innsbruck – one of the top ski-tourism destinations in Austria and where the study took place – students were proud to be able to host and show friends and relatives around the city. Students' activities and spending changed significantly when they were hosting friends. Nightclubbing, attending concerts, biking and skiing were organised with friends and meant an extra outlay for hosts and guests. While students hosting relatives acted as local guides and organised sightseeing tours, parents usually paid for dinners and cultural activities. The authors argue that this youth tourism segment should receive more attention from destination management organisations because students were proud and passionate ambassadors of the city in which they were studying and VFR tourism occurs off-season.

Significantly, most literature on international student mobility focuses on the personal growth of young people without migration backgrounds. In the next section we will consider student mobility and its benefits and challenges, as perceived by migrant-background students.

2.4. Interactions With Culturally Similar Individuals: African-Background Students' Trips 'Home'

A considerable proportion of immigrant youth in EU elementary and secondary schools travel to their or their parents' country of origin at least annually; however, African-background students' trips 'home' are largely neglected in tourism research. An important research project on youth mobility – 'Mobility Trajectories of Young Lives (MO-TRAYL)' – reveals an unexplored issue related to youth student mobility and its consequences for the educational trajectories of migrant-background students (https://www.motrayl.com/). The project investigated the personal impact of trips made to Ghana by young people resident in Belgium both of whose parents were born in Ghana. The authors – Anschütz and Mazzucato (2022) – applied a personal growth lens and examined the ways in which travelling to the country of origin of their (grand)parents influenced their educational achievements. In Selby's (2021) proposed 'Place Practice Model of Mobile Student Experience' identity and place influence one another in a circular process and, according to Selby, the circuit between place and identity represents the rational and reflective components of mobile student experiences. Data were collected over an 18-month period of ethnographic fieldwork in Antwerp and in Ghana. The interviews with 25 young people (aged 14–25) revealed that travelling to Ghana increased their self-confidence and sense of self-efficacy regarding their academic achievements, largely because they felt that they had been able to leave their 'immigrant identity' behind. In some higher educational settings, African-background students still face stereotyping, discrimination and anti-immigrant sentiments. One interviewee said that travelling to Ghana was like 'taking a vacation from the world' (Anschütz & Mazzucato, 2022, p. 7). These are valuable dimensions of young tourists' experiences. Chimamanda Ngozi Adichie, the world-famous writer born and brought up in Nigeria, said in an interview that she first recognised her 'black identity' when she travelled to the USA. Being black in Nigeria was, of course, not an issue. Similarly, one of the Ghanaian-background students interviewed by Anschütz and Mazzucato said that the experience of not being identified by her skin colour in her parents' country of origin made her more self-confident when she returned to Belgium. When young people travel to their (grand)parents' country of origin they establish personal connections with the country, its culture and values and are often prompted to reflect on their own identities.

Anschütz and Mazzucato (2022, p. 5) refer to this phenomenon as the 'multi-local embeddedness of mobile youth' and reveal how the personal growth mechanisms of young people with migration backgrounds differ from those of international students and tourists. The importance that these authors give to 'place' can be usefully connected to Selby's (2021) place-identity circular model. The 'travel-induced personal growth' of Anschütz and Mazzucato's interviewees is not a result of discovering new cultures and people; instead it is about feeling at home and being seen without discrimination and learning (more) about the historic Ghanaian figures who are perceived as role models for the young. These experiences, and the stronger sense of identity and self-efficacy that they nurture, can be capitalised upon to overcome obstacles when the young people return to Europe. Despite the fact that, as the authors point out, institutions and teachers often consider these home-country trips to be academically disruptive, tourism undoubtedly plays a significant role in young people's personal and educational development.

2.5. Interactions With Older People: Religious Tourism and Pilgrimage

We will now turn to contemporary youth pilgrimage, along with the motivational, behavioural and experiential components that determine the influence of tourism on young people's personal development (Olsen, 2022). Studying intergenerational interactions between religious tourists sheds light on young tourists' motivations and behaviour. Today, teens and emerging adults in Western countries are growing up in an era when religion and religious affiliations are questioned (Polus & Carr, 2022). The salience of religious identity predicts time spent on religious activities, and as Timothy and Olsen (2006) claimed young tourists seek pure and cathartic experiences. Contemporary pilgrimage experiences are often transformative for young people (Olsen, 2022). This transformation occurs at different times, in different places. Change is an internal, emotional journey for the pilgrim while s/he is physically and mentally focused on the pilgrimage route and the people s/he encounters. Transformation also comes from without, through encounters and interactions with other pilgrims. Going on pilgrimage is a kind of 'archetype journey' which will, it is hoped, reach and involve the pilgrim's inner centre, their thoughts and beliefs about everything, including the meaning of life and humans' role and place on Earth (Timothy & Olsen, 2006). Young tourists have different motivations for going on pilgrimage. To cover the 800 km Camino to Santiago de Compostela (Spain) on foot or by bicycle is a sporting achievement which can be sufficient motivation for going on that particular pilgrimage.

However, pilgrimage-journeys always involve self-reflection and spiritual trans-formation, whatever the pilgrim's principal motivation initially. Woodside and Megehee (2010) showed that pilgrims' accounts of their journeys can represent a veritable treasure chest of their motivations and behaviour. In this regard, consider the following Image 2 and the insight by a 22-year-old pilgrim on her way to Santiago de Compostela.

Image 2.   A Pilgrim on One of the Most Popular Pilgrimage Routes in Europe, El Camino.

When I started the journey, it was purely for the desire for adventure. I would have never imagined that I would live my once-in-a-lifetime experience. I got to know the person closest to heart, myself. The path gave me much more than just cultural enrichment. Gratitude. Courage. Self-knowledge. Freedom. (Courtesy by: Zsofi, Fekete, photo by Daniel Puskás)

Intergenerational encounters in religious tourism have been studied by Irimiás et al. (2018), drawing on the legend of the Quest for the Holy Grail to understand the religious experiences of both old and young tourists in their interconnectedness. In the legend, an old king lives in a wasteland. Wounded and ill, he is waiting for a young person to whom he can entrust the Holy Grail, the mysterious vessel endowed with life-preserving power used by Jesus at the Last Supper. The Grail has been the object of desire of many but can only be touched by the few who are worthy of doing so. The young knight Perceval is sent to save the kingdom and to ask the king the right questions. If he succeeds and attains the Grail, the Fisher King will be safe. Applying this archetype quest to religious tourism experiences and using the metaphor of the 'Fisher King' (a religious tourist aged over 60) and 'Perceval' (18–24 -olds), the researchers collected 151 personal pilgrimage narratives. In their accounts, the young tourists gave particular weight to the powerful experiences that they had had during the pilgrimage, including those shared with old(er) pilgrims (Irimiás et al., 2018, p. 232).

> On the pilgrimage my mother and my mother-in-law changed completely. I saw them rejuvenated even though they were old. I knew how they lived their life at home, they avoided going out because everywhere was crowded, they became tired after a while and they don't like that. But here, on the pilgrimage, both changed completely. To see them changed made me feel really happy. I think it was a good idea to take them on a pilgrimage. (Interview_232)

The authors noted that initially the young Percevals are rather sceptical about their role as companions/helpers and what exactly they mean to their older travel companions (Irimiás et al., 2018, p. 229). In the following extract from an interview, we read about the moment when a young tourist understands that her mere presence is healing for her grandmother. And this moment is transformative for the young woman, as she reflects on self and her identity. Here, the young 'Perceval' is reconsidering her life values:

> If my grandmother had not begged me, probably, I would have never, ever in my life have taken part in a religious event. She used to attend every year with my grandpa when he was still alive; after his death, she used to go with her friends or even alone. I told her on the phone that I would go with her. To hear her happiness made me feel an indescribable joy. She was holding my arm during the whole service and she was smiling at me… and showing gratitude, peacefulness and love. After returning home she started crying and thanked me for sharing that moment with her. She said that the service was a spiritual purification for her. (Interview_138)

The metaphor of a mirror and its reflection is particularly relevant to the experiences of young pilgrims: Perceval and the Fisher King, the helper and the wounded, are interconnected and the experience of one is understood through its reflection in the other. As discussed in Chapter 1, both young and old tourists are often considered to be homogeneous groups and are stereotyped accordingly. Intergenerational communication and interaction at sacred sites are important as the Irimiás et al.'s (2018) study have shown. Pilgrimage and religious tourism experiences are transformative because the participants find themselves in new roles, the old and/or ill are accomplishing something and, in this achievement, regain their status as people to be admired. And young tourist Percevals, too, play new roles, as helpers, co-travellers and healers during the pilgrimage and fellow tourists on returning home.

While considering religious tourism, we must mention the World Youth Days, which celebrate and express trust in the young. World Youth Day (WYD) is an event organised for young people (aged 16–35) by the Catholic Church. Pope John Paul II established WYD with the intention of bringing young Catholics from around the world closer to Christ through this opportunity to pray and celebrate together. In 1986, Rome hosted the first jamboree and since then WYD has been held every three years or so, in different cities (e.g. Buenos Aires, Krakow, Madrid, Panama, and Sydney). The six-day event attracts huge crowds of young people who want to meet the Pope and be part of an international community based on a common set of values and beliefs (https://worldyouthday.com/). The organisation enables participants to travel on a budget; indeed, many pilgrims are hosted by local families, schools or ecclesiastical accommodation services. Pilgrims attend secular and religious activities during the six-day event and enjoy being in a group with others. As I write, WYD organisers are working on the next event to be hosted in Lisbon (Portugal) in 2023. Pope Francis has recently encouraged the world's youth to let their voices be heard and to make 'a noise' about the issues they really care about. The next jamboree, in which hundreds of thousands of young people from all over the world will take part, should be a good occasion to let those voices be heard.

The previous sections focused on education and spiritual journeys, tourism experiences that hold the promise of personal development. In the next section, young tourists' work-travel experiences are briefly analysed. Youth work-travel has evolved a great deal in recent decades in terms of its structure, offers and geographical locations.

2.6. Work-Travel Experiences

Combining travel with paid work, skill development and leisure activities, work-travel experiences are popular among young tourists (Reisinger & Turner, 2011; Richards & Morrill, 2020). A working holiday involves young tourists travelling to engage in some form of short-term service, mostly during their summer holidays (Carr, 1998). The organisations that run work-travel programmes provide young tourists and their families with insurance coverage and some legal assistance and arrange contracts between the parties for accommodation, meals and pocket money. Most offer quality standards, guidance, transparency and 24/7 assistance. The Workaway.com platform offers a wide range of employment possibilities: working for NGOs, on farms, in families, for boat owners who need help maintaining or even crewing their craft – the possibilities are endless. Young tourists interested in sustainable agriculture can also join the Worldwide Opportunities on Organic Farms (WWOOF) – a UK-based educational and cultural exchange programme to promote organic farming and sustainability, with members in 130 countries – and volunteer (for anything from one day to several months) on an organic farm. House-sitting is another way for the young to work and travel on a budget. Duties usually involve simply looking after houses and any pets while their owners are away.

Working as an au-pair provides another popular opportunity to travel (Bagnoli, 2009). Foreign au-pairs can work on tourist visas; they stay with a family for a certain period and help to look after the children. Young (18–25-year old) females are the target market for organisations connecting *au-pairs* with potential host families. One well-known platform is aupairworld.com, a member of the World Youth Student and Educational Travel Confederation (WYSE). The market is huge – according to the latest figures published by Au-pair World, in June 2021, the four-millionth user registered on their website (www.aupairworld.com). The most popular *au-pair* destinations are Australia, Europe, Japan, New Zealand and the USA. In order to avoid the problems which can arise if *au-pairs* without any childcare experience or skills are hired, responsibilities and expectations (on both sides) must be clearly defined in advance. Indeed, working as an au-pair can have its disadvantages: the job (almost always) involves domestic chores; talking primarily to children rather than to adults so that the former can learn whatever language the au-pair speaks; it may also mean spending a lot of time alone.

As discussed previously, most higher education institutions encourage students to find (generally four to six months) internships abroad. There is usually a formal agreement between the hosting workplace and the student's place of education which awards credits for the internship. Young people are motivated to participate in 'work and travel' experiences for similar reasons to those making study abroad programmes attractive: the opportunity to travel, to learn/improve a foreign language, to establish new relationships, to gain experience in an intercultural environment and to enhance their CVs (Lejealle et al., 2021).

While sending children and adolescents to overseas summer camps has become quite a common practice for middle-class European and Chinese families, these summer camps also provide valuable work and travel opportunities for young tourists. Research on emerging adults employed as counsellors at overnight (residential) summer camps has shown that they were actively exploring – and hence developing – their identities. In interviews with 20 counsellors (aged 18–22) from eight summer camps in New England, it was found that the experience of performing different roles – caregiver, friend, entertainer, facilitator, etc. – in the camp was a transformative experience. Identity exploration involves identifying the goals, values, and beliefs that you are committed to. The camp environment allowed these young people to explore and express different aspects of their identity. A culture of acceptance encouraged them to 'be themselves', and the mix of adult- and child-appropriate tasks gave them the opportunity to experience a variety of roles and responsibilities. Such opportunities are not always provided by universities or colleges.

A study by Povilaitis and Tamminen (2018) confirms the above findings that summer camps can contribute to personal development. According to these authors, this development is, above all, the fruit of the relationships formed between campers and leaders, and between campers and the surrounding environment, over prolonged periods of intensive interaction. Residential summer sports camps in particular can nurture personal development because they provide the eight settings features: (1) physical and psychological safety, (2) appropriate structure, (3) supportive relationships, (4) opportunities to belong, (5) positive social norms, (6) support for efficacy and mattering, (7) opportunities for skill building and (8) integration of family, school and community efforts. The interviews with 30 counsellors and coaches (aged 20–28) revealed that leaders' supportive relations with campers played an essential role in personal development with camp staff acting as mentors or role models for younger campers. Campers are encouraged to leave their comfort zones and to engage in active learning activities with peers. Interestingly, coaches and counsellors also personally experience positive development, indicating that these interactions are mutually beneficial. As parents do not tend to be involved in camp programmes, however, the last feature (the integration of family, school and community efforts) is not easily achievable.

2.7. Volunteer Tourism

A growing body of research exists on volunteer tourism (McGehee, 2012; McGehee & Andereck, 2009; Wearing, 2001). Originally, volunteer experiences were managed by religious institutions, youth clubs and non-government organisations (NGOs) and required detailed planning, intense preparation and committed volunteers. Today, it is difficult to estimate the size of the global volunteer tourism market, some sources mention 4 million (www.volunteerworld.com), others 10 million (www.cbi.eu), *voluntourists* ('volunteer' and 'tourist') a year. Purposeful travellers can choose to go to any one of the 80 countries in which projects are located. Activities range from building dog shelters, to teaching English, to giving medical assistance. Volunteering abroad has been popular in the Scandinavian countries, the UK and the USA since the 1980s, and recently significant numbers of young people from Asian and African countries have been applying to volunteer programmes.

The *voluntourist* has been defined as someone who utilises their discretional time and income to travel a long distance with the intention of doing some good and assisting others in need (McGehee & Santos, 2005; Wearing, 2001). Voluntourists are of all ages, but the majority are young. They usually cover their own expenses, work on a project without remuneration and collaborate with members of the host community. While they sometimes organise their own journeys, many rely on organisations and associations that function as voluntourism intermediaries. Most projects are organised by international/local NGOs and accept volunteers for anything from a few days to a year or more. Volunteers usually travel abroad, for short periods, and join (working) groups. Although voluntourism is about project work, NGOs generally do not require any specific knowledge, training or skills. While this approach gives young people a chance to test themselves, doing something that they are passionate about (wildlife conservation, organic farming, sports coaching, etc.), it also involves risk, particularly in terms of the quality of the service provided by volunteers. School rooms built by voluntourists may have safety issues, English language courses taught by young adults with no teaching qualifications or experience have questionable results and the efficacy of untrained volunteers working on wildlife/animal protection projects is also doubtful. McGehee and Andereck's (2009) insightful research evidenced these mixed results and called for further investigation of the power relations between host communities (referred to as being 'voluntoured') and tourists. McGehee (2012, p. 91) later suggested applying Foucauldian critical theory to explore

> the volunteer tourist-volunteer tour organization-host relation-ship as a potential form of resistance to the dominant-subordinate dichotomy relationship whereby the tourist possesses socially and historically constituted power over the host community.

Research shows that voluntourism is highly popular among the young who believe volunteering to be a catalyst for social change; this perception has led volunteering with humanitarian or nature preservation organisations to gain prestige. While voluntourism is a consciousness-raising experience because volun-teers are directly involved in complex socio-economic (and political) issues, it also 'serves as a stronghold for the privileged' (McGehee, 2012, p. 93) and strengthens established power/knowledge relations between locals and young tourists.

The idea of visiting countries like Ecuador, Costa Rica, South Africa or Nepal, etc., appeals to young tourists. Volunteering on a project for a fortnight costs, on average, $2,000. A shift in the narrative discourse of volunteer tourism is evident in more recent studies: young voluntourists' motivations appear to have changed, and while they still want to go on a 'meaningful journey', we find that the primary tourism motivations now are to strengthen one's CV by providing evidence of commitment to a cause, to have an adventure, to gain information/knowledge, to develop a skill set, to build a network and to establish friendships.

Early research on volunteer tourism studied tourists' motivations and found that altruism, civic responsibility, the wish to give something back and to help those in need inspired young people to volunteer abroad (Heuman, 2005; Pearce & Coghlan, 2008; Wearing, 2001). These studies showed that volunteer experiences were transformative both for young tourists and host communities and proposed that cross-cultural settings often made interactions more meaning-ful and reduced prejudice and stereotypes (McGehee, 2012). Voluntourism was believed to benefit both the host society and the tourist. While some volunteer tourism organisations are driven by locals and genuinely endeavour to foster residents' emancipation, other organisations increase power inequality. Recent research on this topic has revealed that some organisations have commercialised and commodified volunteer tourism with terrible consequences for local commu-nities, particularly children.

Feminist criticism of voluntourists questions the moral commitment, altruism and legitimacy of female volunteer tourists who display their experiences – and, above all, themselves – while doing volunteer work. Wearing et al. (2018) concep-tualised this phenomenon and explored the social media critique on the behav-iour of white, wealthy female tourists in their 20s – the ironically called Barbie saviours. It appeared that these 'volunteers' primary motivation was to share self-ies and videos on social media and thus to display their volunteering experience. Similarly, Woods and Shee (2021) found that the role of social media, in particular Instagram, was paramount in Singaporean volunteers' decisions about where to travel and what to do. Community service is compulsory in Singapore's education system and voluntourism trips to neighbouring countries – Cambodia, Indonesia, Thailand and Vietnam – are organised for students. Conducting 20 interviews with young volunteers and analysing the images posted on social media, the authors investigated how humanitarian projects, such as Holiday for Humanity in South East Asia, can turn into a veritable showground for young female influencers and their followers. The real motivation of these young 'humanitarian volunteers' was self-promotion, and they used their voluntourism experiences to create photos and videos to post on Instagram.

2.8. Volunteering at Sporting Events

Sport events are often primary attractions to young tourists. Young sport fans usually consider that it is worth saving money to be able to watch a match in one of the iconic stadiums in the world. An important work-travel tourism phenomenon is to travel to a mega sporting event to participate as a volunteer. Indeed, volunteer tourists at sporting events contribute significantly to the success of the event. Working for a mega sporting event is prestigious; the Olympic games recruit volunteers from all over the world. The Sydney 2000 and Athens 2004 Olympics relied on more than 40,000 volunteers, and Beijing 2008 had 100,000. Candidates are invited to apply years ahead of the event. Research indicates that volunteer tourists at mega sporting events recall their experience in favourable terms, highlighting the positive life experience and social enrichment. Volunteer tourists with positive experiences are usually keen to participate in other volunteer tourism programmes, as anticipated by social exchange theory which posits that perceived costs and benefits associated with a certain behaviour can predict the repetition of that behaviour in the future. Ralston et al. (2005) surveyed 1,100 volunteers at the XII Commonwealth Games in Manchester (UK) in 2002. Excitement, making the most of a once-in-a-lifetime opportunity, meeting people, supporting sport, giving back to the community and helping the city were volunteers' main motivations. The authors found that megasporting events are particularly significant for young tourists and are also a way to enhance community development. Volunteering has also been recognised as a potential way to contribute to the successful implementation of the Agenda 2030 Sustainable Development Goal of guaranteeing decent employment and working opportunities for young people. And finally, having volunteered – and being able to add the experience to your CV – can benefit young tourists as they begin their working lives.

2.9. Travelling to Learn (Gap Years and Backpackers)

A 'gap year', a break in one's study/career trajectory (as distinct from an annual holiday), is prevalently a Western concept and phenomenon (Bagnoli, 2009; Pearce & Foster, 2007). Generally defined as a year-long period of experiential learning and travelling, the phenomenon gained popularity in the 1980s. Originally, the term 'gap year' or 'year out' referred to a period of time when young people combined different activities such as paid/volunteer work, leisure and travelling before beginning university (Jones, 2004).

Pearce and Foster (2007) called the gap year, and backpacking during it, 'the university of travel' on account of the formative and learning experiences that such journeys provide. These holidays, which constitute a disjunction in a linear career path, have been popular among young people in the UK, Ireland, Scandinavia and Israel since 1980s (Noy & Cohen, 2005). In Central and Eastern European countries, it used to be incomprehensible to most that young people were allowed to take time out from their career and to travel. In New Zealand, the so-called 'Overseas Experience' (OE) is undertaken by many young people in their 20s and is regarded as a rite of passage into adulthood. Although OEs are characterised by fun, and hedonistic experiences, most people value them above all for the sense of freedom and personal development that they allow. As Bagnoli (2009, p. 331) remarked of the gap year, this contemporary 'educational trip has nowadays become a middle-class ritual', responding to young people's need for self-development. The same can, of course, be said of the OE. We should remember, however, that parents and families are (almost always) involved in decision-making around what to do and where to go. As mentioned at the beginning of the chapter, the notion that extended trips abroad can help people to grow up and become autonomous and interculturally competent was already accepted in the era of the Grand Tour. The gap year/OE has gained new meanings as young tourists from other locations have started to take a year out, interrupting their education and career trajectories. Underlying these decisions is the idea that travelling for an extended period of time can significantly enhance young people's soft and hard skills and make them more mature and independent (O'Reilly, 2006).

Wu and Pearce (2018) coined the term 'gap time' in order to distinguish the concept from the Western 'gap year' and have highlighted the impressive size and potential of the Chinese youth travel market, while noting that the idea of a 'gap year' is little known (and not encouraged) in China. It is important to understand the perceived benefits of 'gap time', its 'worthiness' as well as the travel constraints on Chinese youth travel. The priorities, concerns and values of the young Chinese do not necessarily align with those of their Western contemporaries. Findings show that they prefer to take relatively short breaks during their early career. Some of the constraints that they experience are the same as those faced by young Westerners: time, money, no one to travel with. Other issues are more specific to their cultural milieu: certain social responsibilities, parental constraints, safety concerns and competing interests (Xie, 2022). Taking a 'gap year' has been uncommon and can be considered to deviate from the defined and expected career trajectories in China. As everywhere, in China cultural values shape society and condition the behaviours of young and old alike. Chinese society is, of course, collectivist, social relations are shaped by 'guanxi', social networks that determine the present and future actions of individuals and communities. For young Chinese, taking some 'gap time' – an apparently individualistic decision – risks disappointing others. In fact, fear of losing face because of a behaviour considered 'deviant' places considerable constraints on Chinese 'gap time'. However, giving Chinese youth the opportunity to take some 'gap time' could, on the one hand, have a positive impact on the management of educational and employment systems within China. On the other hand, moreover, adapting to a new market segment consisting of young Chinese in their 'gap time' could change South-eastern Asian countries and Australia's destination marketing communication.

2.10. Backpackers

In a recent study, Timothy and Zhu (2022) reflect on the temporal, spatial and cultural perspectives of backpacker tourism, with a focus on the young. Backpacking tourism 'is generally characterized by independent, low-budget forms of travel in which people overnight in low-cost accommodations, such as campgrounds, hostels, homestays and, more recently, CouchSurfing and shared Airbnb rentals' (Timothy & Zhu, 2022, p. 250). Today, most backpackers travel with their smartphones and a good internet connection is a priority. Unlocked portable routers, USB dongles and eSIM cards are must-have objects for staying in constant contact with home and maintaining one's presence on social media platforms. Backpackers tend to use public transport, enjoy street food (or cook their own) and stay in less energy-intensive accommodation structures than mass tourists and therefore to have smaller environmental footprints (Martins & Costa, 2022).

According to Pearce and Foster (2007, p. 1285), backpacking

> delineates the activities and products of a mobile, usually younger market segment who exhibit a preference for budget accommodation, emphasise meeting other travellers, follow an independently organised and flexible travel schedule, pursue longer rather than very brief holidays and prefer informal and participatory holiday activities.

Some backpackers are also keen hikers, an activity which requires physical fitness, determination and careful planning. No hike along the Appalachian Trail, the longest hiking-only trail in the world, could be accomplished without planning, organisation and commitment. This 2,194 mile (circa 3,530 km) trail crosses 14 states, from Georgia to Maine, and is one of the most scenic hiking trails in the USA, a dream hike for many backpackers, as are the Pacific Crest Trail and the Continental Divide Trail. To cover the full length of the trail takes about six months and those who succeed in this endeavour are called 'thru-hikers'. Thru-hikers' social identity is formed within the community they belong to, hikers meet their fellows on the trail and many feel as though they belong to a trail family (the 'tramily') with whom they hike and camp. A person's social identity is their sense of belonging to a social group, a set of like-minded individuals who view themselves as members of the same social category (Stryker & Burke, 2000). Young adults often define themselves in relation to their peers by perceiving similarities and differences between themselves and other group members. Self-categorisation refers to the accentuation of such similarities and/or differences in beliefs, values, attitudes and affective reactions. Backpackers' social identity becomes tangible through their equipment: backpack, tent, sleeping bag, hammock, dehydrated meals, etc. The market for these products is robust, and companies invest in innovation and product development to meet backpackers' consumer needs.

Backpacking is an enriching life experience. In our highly individualised society backpacking is often perceived as a way to 'find oneself': a – usually brief – window of opportunity free from social obligations. As mentioned before, backpacking has been called the 'university of Travel'. Pearce and Foster (2007) employed a quantitative method with a sample of 372 backpackers and used a 42-item checklist of generic skills in a survey to explore what backpackers had learnt through their travel experiences. And, according to the interviewees, they had acquired self-confidence, tolerance and independence and improved their planning, organisational, communication and decision-making skills during their journeys.

Returning to China, Zhang et al.'s (2018) study on 'backpackers' identity' provides intriguing insights into how Chinese backpackers adapt their self-definition meanings to the situations that they find themselves in. The authors found that Chinese backpackers identify themselves as a social category, whereas Western backpackers identify themselves by their behaviour. It is important to consider the growing phenomenon of Chinese backpackers as a reflection of current social change in China, where young travellers are referred to as members of the post-80s generation. Different types of 'life-style' mobility have emerged in China in recent decades (Xie, 2022). The need to know oneself better and the desire to enhance competences and gain new skills and to establish social relations have made backpacking popular among young Chinese tourists. Xie (2022, p. 5) highlights the importance of situating the latter's backpacker experiences within their wider life experiences. She interviewed several Chinese backpackers about their motivations for travelling and discovered that they saw travelling independently, rather than on a package tour, as a privilege reserved for young professionals and college students. Chinese backpackers, however, rarely travel alone. Cai (2018) has argued that backpacking needs to be reconceptualised from a Chinese perspective. In China, 'donkey friends' (驴友 lü you), backpackers who search for a travel companion online, have become increasingly popular. Calling a backpacker a 'donkey friend' is a play on words – the Chinese words for 'donkey friends' and 'travel' are homophones. Cai (2018) argued that young Chinese backpackers are tech-savvy and have bigger budgets but less annual leave than their Western counterparts. As mentioned above, Chinese society is collectivist, and the popularity of finding a travel companion online can be explained by people's high sensitivity to risk, their wish to avoid loneliness overseas and a need to stay within their budget. These are the main motivations for creating a small, culturally homogeneous travel group with strangers and going on a long-haul journey together. Of course, the Covid-19 pandemic has – for now – completely changed this situation: travel in and out of China is, at the time of writing, severely restricted and extremely expensive. For more on backpacker tourists see Martins and Costa's (2022) volume in this book series.

2.11. Conclusions

In this chapter, we considered youth tourism from the personal growth perspective and investigated tourists' travel career patterns to understand their motivations (Pearce, 2022). Emerging adulthood (Arnett, 2016) is a key period in identity formation during which individuals reflect on their role(s) in society and on themselves. Identity is multifaceted and people possess different identities in different social contexts, each identity is thus influenced by social structures and interactions with others. Tourism is such a broad field that it lends itself well to the exploration of diverse social contexts such as education and learning, work, volunteer experiences and participation in religious events. Personal development is a long process shaped by the people and situations that we encounter. Interacting with people from a different ethnic, cultural or social background – and reflecting on these experiences – can contribute to developing one's intercultural sensitivity. Tourism encounters may contribute to the understanding that one's worldview is a cultural construct. African-background students' sense of identity and belonging is enhanced by the experience of travelling to their or their (grand) parents' country of origin. While in Ghana, these young tourists could leave their 'immigrant identity' behind. When travelling with old(er) companions – in the contexts we have discussed, on pilgrimage or at religious events – young people often find themselves in situations in which they are called upon to act as Percevals. Volunteer and backpacker tourism have long been associated with youth tourism, and these experiences are – to varying degrees – transformative. Future research is needed to discover the long-term impact of these experiences on tourists' lives and identity formation.

Chapter 3

The Young Tourist and Hedonistic Experiences

Hedonistic experiences and intimacy are primordial human needs which influence (to varying extents) young tourists' behaviour. Festival and pop-culture tourism are assessed in the pages that follow, taking into account the importance of belonging and self-actualisation. While not exhaustive, the chapter will map out a range of activities for young tourists and the meanings that participants attach to their experiences. As Khoo-Lattimore and Ling (2018, p.7) observe, youth leisure market consumers are often seen as 'young, independent and adventurous visitors'. That said, being young is also, for many, a continuous struggle between being independent and preserving social bonds and being adventurous – even wild – and taking quiet time out to reflect on deeper questions such as who one is and where one is going. Foucault's (1986) concept of heterotopia is used here to understand the spaces of leisure. Youth tourism is approached as a social practice and the wide spectrum of youth tourism motivations, attitudes and behaviours is presented in order to stimulate further research in the field. Before discussing young tourists' hedonistic experiences, it is important to briefly mention young people as protagonists in family holidays.

3.1. Young Tourists on Family Holidays

Young tourists should never be seen as desocialised tourist subjects. Inevitably, tourism trends in general and tourist behaviour specifically are shaped by social change. However, much of the tourism literature is consumer and target segment-driven and, when investigating young tourists' attitudes, preferences and behaviours, tends to do so as if these manifest in a social bubble. Young tourists move and act within their own particular social circle, influence and are influenced by their social contacts and relationships and behave in ways that are largely shaped by the people and situations that they encounter. As discussed in Chapter 1, many young adults still live at home for a variety of reasons. In five OECD countries, in 2019, more than 50 per cent of young people (between the ages of 15 and 29) were living at home: 81 per cent of young Italians, 76 per cent of young Greeks,

The Youth Tourist: Motives, Experiences and Travel Behaviour, 45–62
Copyright © 2023 by Anna Irimiás
Published under exclusive licence by Emerald Publishing Limited
doi:10.1108/978-1-80455-147-920231004

74 per cent of young Spaniards, 56 per cent of young Germans and 67 per cent of young people in the USA (Statista, 2020). This situation influences the tourism decision-making and behaviour of both families as a unit and individual young people. Millennial parents travel with very young children; it is not uncommon to see babies and toddlers on long-haul flights or in the family zones of international trains. As adults, these children will be experienced tourists. Youth tourists travel alone, with friends and also with parents and other family members. Longer transitions to adulthood and more multigenerational households are directly effecting tourism behaviour in general. The structure of US families, one of the most important tourism source countries, has witnessed a significant transformation. Young adults are much more likely to accept having to live in multigenerational households than five decades ago (Pew Research Center, 2022). Some family nests may not empty for years, and family members in multigenerational households can be predicted to travel together.

Family holidays are about social connection and togetherness rather than escape from everyday life. Teenagers and young adults in Western countries have grown up in more egalitarian societies than their forebearers, and this societal change has also shaped family structures and values. While some tourism advertising still employs the image of the 'ideal' nuclear family of four (mother, father, daughter, son), most tourism planners and advertisers have recognised that many people now live in plural family settings (single-parent families, divorced or blended families, LGBTQIA+ families, etc.). These evolving relationships and interactions between family members have an impact on youth tourism. Schänzel et al. (2012, p.4) define family holidays as 'purposive time spent together as a family group (which may include extended family) doing activities different from normal routines that are fun but that may involve compromise and conflict at times'. This definition encapsulates the essence of family trips: having fun together but also feeling limited in the kinds of individual decisions one can take. Anyone who has ever travelled with a teenager will recognise this ambivalence. Research indicates that teens constitute a significant share of the family holiday market. Young people are effective persuaders and greatly influence adult spending; moreover, parents often want to give their children an opportunity to learn directly and experientially about a particular city and its culture (Webster, 2012). On family holidays, children's curiosity and enthusiasm about experiential activities usually draw the whole family in and when, during the trip, children learn about a destination, they engage more readily in the holiday experience. Parents and caregivers want their children to have a positive holiday experience, to create travel memories and – in the case of most families – to learn something from their travels. Many families in Western countries put a high value on the family holiday. Webster (2012) suggests that young audiences should be directly targeted in tourism marketing communications and destination promotion should emphasise participatory and experiential offers. The following photo and its description, in a young Italian tourist's own words, give us an insight into her experience of travelling with her father (Image 1).

Young tourists often feel the need to reconnect with family members and friends and to celebrate milestone events such as weddings, graduation

Image 1.   Travelling With Parents, Naples (Italy).
My father took this picture of me during our trip to Naples. It is a very spontaneous picture because I did not ask him to take it, he just wanted to capture the magic of the Neapolitan alleys with all their vibrant colours and ancient stones. When I saw the picture, I really liked it because it reminded me of the soul of Naples, a city with hundreds of hidden treasures that can be discovered at every corner. I posted this picture on my Instagram page because it shows the authenticity of that travel experience for me. My father and I walked miles and miles to find new landscapes and artistic glimpses and I was amazed by the richness of beauty of Naples. The welcoming lights, the warm colours, the narrow streets, this picture just captures the essence of Naples. (Courtesy by: Nicole Betta, 2022)

ceremonies or the births of children together. Some psychologists describe these 'transformative experiences' as life-altering or turning points in one's life. These turning points are particularly important in young people's lives. School holidays also give families a chance to travel and thus celebrate holidays together. Christmas, Thanksgiving, Chinese New Year and the important Hindu festivals are all occasions when young adults travel to be with their families and friends. Some important research on young Chinese adults' family holidays gives us a new angle on youth tourists' travel motivations. Employing netnography to Chinese travel blogs, Wang et al. (2018) investigated what motivated young adults to go on holiday with their parents. The authors discovered that Confucian ethics, a sense of family duty and adult children's desire to give back were the primary motivations. Bloggers also reported that they had long been planning to take their parents – many of whom had never travelled before – on holiday.

So, many of these trips were organised by the young adults as a gift to their parents. Going on holiday together meant a lot to the young adults and gave them joy because it enabled them to spend valuable time together, reward their parents, express filial piety and enjoy themselves.

3.2. Hedonistic Holiday Experiences (4-S and Winter Tourism)

Hedonistic leisure activities make tourists feel good but can also be meaningful. Youth tourism is often an opportunity for experiences; for many young tourists these trips are the first time that they have stepped out of their everyday routines and into a fluid, temporary space. Hedonistic pleasure is often experienced in liminal tourism spaces which may well have their own social norms. The terms liminal and liminoid need to be distinguished, and the concept of liminoid refers to an in-between state in which social rules do not seem to apply (Sharpley, 2022).

The notion of play is also key to understanding liminal tourism experiences. This is closely linked to what Turner conceptualised as a rite of passage, involving different stages:

(1) the separation phase, the initial departure from home;
(2) the transition in which playfulness and fun-seeking characterise many young tourists' behaviour; and
(3) the incorporation phase, in which the young tourist is reintegrated with his/ her social group.

Many young people's experience of being on holiday is quite simply relishing the feeling that they do not have to study or work; their holiday behaviour involves clubbing and consuming alcohol and/or drugs, just like when they go out at home. During the late 1980s and 1990s, the importance of the night-club scene in holiday destinations increased as more and more tour operators exploited the demands of the youth tourism market (Shaw & Williams, 2004). Until recently, clubbing destinations have been aggressively marketed to attract young tourists with the promise of a hedonistic holiday in places in which social rules and norms do not seem to apply. In relation to youth tourism, it is crucial to understand what happens and why it happens in nightlife (urban/seaside) destinations. Sönmez et al. (2013, p.34) defined clubbing tourists as

> sensation-seeking youth travellers primarily between the ages of 18 and 26 who follow DJs and MCs to various nightlife resort destinations at peak season to stay from one to two weeks. Their main goal is to drink, party, and enjoy the sun for as little cost as possible.

In fact, risky drinking practices such as binge drinking and pregaming (drinking large amount of alcohol in a very short time) are common. Shaw and Williams (2004, p.151) argue that the norms of holiday behaviour become very different from other patterns of behaviour. Such ludic or playful behaviour is seen by some as restitutive or compensatory, making up for home and work routines.

Party-holidaying can be seen as taking time out to withdraw from social norms in a place that is not home. As social learning theory posits, people tend to mimic others in certain situations. Transformative experiences are more likely in contexts where the social norms accepted in a tourist's home environment carry little – or even, sometimes, no – weight.

Young tourists' hedonistic activities are linked to the concept of the 'pleasure periphery'. Some of the holiday destinations where young people can engage in activities outside the norm include the Mediterranean region, the Caribbean and Southeast Asia. Selänniemi (2003) argues that 4-S (sea, sand, sun and sex) destinations are located in the pleasure periphery where freedom from responsibility and transgressions in terms of time, space, mind and senses are possible. Young tourists' perception of the pleasure periphery as a tolerant space, combined with its festive atmosphere, may give them licence – and the confidence – to experiment sexually in their choice of partners and the nature of their encounters.

In these reinvented seaside resorts and places, extreme forms of consumption and behaviour with a mixture of sex, alcohol and drugs can be witnessed. Experiences in the pleasure periphery may involve varying degrees of moral inversion and the (ab)use of bodies, sexualities and pleasure (Mitev, 2007a, 2007b). The concept of the 'dirty weekend' has been used in relation to the transgressive behaviour of people who feel as though they are 'out of time, place and mind' (Pritchard & Morgan, 2006, p.764). The promise of hedonistic experiences, combined with alcohol and/or drug consumption, motivates some young people to travel to 4S destinations (Sönmez et al., 2013). Some mature sun and sea destinations have invested in the creation of a destination image in which nightlife is paramount.

During the Covid-19 pandemic 4-S destinations such as Lloret de Mar in Spain and the Greek party islands were very badly affected by the absence of tourists. Then, when air travel started up again and travel restrictions were lifted, herds of young tourists flocked to 'sun lust destinations' with their often highly permissive atmospheres. An accelerated transgression and contestation of everyday social norms allows young tourists to live in suspended time, place and mind. Young adults' perceptions of sexual risk are very likely to be affected by the different – much less inhibited – environment that they find themselves in. These risks include not only sexually transmitted infections but also emotional, mental and social harms. Marin et al. (2021) have shown that Lloret de Mar, which received about 1.3 million tourists with 5.8 million overnight stays before the Covid-19 pandemic, has been strategic in repositioning its brand away from the club scene, thereby attracting (previously untapped) cultural and business tourist segments to the destination. The Destination Management Organisation in Mallorca (Spain) recently decided to limit transgressive (booze) party tourism on the island; in the summer of 2022, the city's municipality purchased some pubs and nightclubs in order to then close them down. On occasion, conflicts arise between young tourists whose motivations are incompatible.

Much of the existing tourism literature on sexualised places has focused on 'sun lust destinations' and beaches (Andriotis, 2010). However, urban and even mountain tourism environments also need to be taken into account when considering sexually permissive atmospheres; the cities so popular for hen and stag parties, for instance (Harris et al., 2022), which are usually characterised by excessive alcohol consumption, transgressive behaviour and activities that go against accepted social norms. Low-cost flights within Europe have made many of the continent's cities and their vibrant nightlife and clubbing scenes easily accessible, even to young adults with relatively limited budgets. As Prentice (2004, p. 262) pointed out, 'anxious, competitive and bored young adults are often protagonists of urban night life' and all too frequently engage in risky behaviours which can lead to serious injuries or even death. Media coverage highlighting the risks of sex parties, drugs, binge drinking competitions, etc. has made these partying youths in nightlife resorts or urban destinations notorious.

Winter sports tourism is very popular among young tourists, many of whom are attracted to Alpine destinations with their world-famous ski slopes, stunning mountain scenery and opportunities to potentially excel in various winter sports. Winter tourism is also about hedonistic holiday experiences and ski chalets give young tourists a chance to experience *communitas* with like-minded skiers. Conviviality, sharing stories and a sense of adventure and achievement, these are a big part of young tourists' winter tourism experiences and are among the most significant push factors for them. Chalet life and après-ski experiences are particularly popular. McLeay et al. (2019) carried out an ethnographic study of a typically British tourism product, the all-inclusive ski-chalet holiday in an Alpine ski resort. In this longitudinal study, 26 of the 37 skiers interviewed were young tourists; their reflections on the meanings that they attribute to the ski-chalet tourism experience are reported in the study. These include the importance of forming and strengthening *communitas*, of being able to socialise and participate in a ski-chalet community, and their enjoyment of the all-inclusive chalet offering, active outdoor experiences and the co-creation of experiences with peers and the chalet staff.

3.3. Young Tourists, Sex, Intimacy

Young people's attitudes to intimacy and sexual relationships in their everyday lives cannot be neatly separated from how they feel when on holiday or while travelling.

In Western countries, young people's attitudes to romantic, intimate relationships and the concept of dating have changed rapidly over recent decades, and many young adults no longer prioritise committed/long-term relationships as previous generations did. Recent research in sociology has revealed that many young people prefer 'situationships' – defined as fluid intimate contacts that sit somewhere between friendship and sexual relationship – to committed relationships. In a 2022 BBC interview, the sociologist Elizabeth Armstrong said that 'right now, [a situationship] solves some kind of need for sex, intimacy, companionship—whatever it is – but this does not have, necessarily, a long-term time horizon'. Until recently, for women staying in an uncommitted relationship was considered to be a waste of time. In contemporary society, the young do not feel the urge (or cannot afford) to settle down and therefore situationships are not perceived negatively as relationships which are going nowhere, that is, have no *future*, but positively as relationships which make both people feel good *in the present*. Situationships – across sexual orientations, genders and ethnicities – are predicated on a liquid understanding of intimate relationships and the need for sex, but do not imply any intention to create a life-long bond. Women who enter into situationships argue that they are thus able to maintain their autonomy, whereas committed relationships are time-consuming and a long-term/committed partner can sometimes limit one's freedom or even try to control one.

Changes in sexual behaviour need to be contextualised. Committed, long-term relationships were not always prioritised by young people in the 1960s and 1970s either. In fact, open and/or casual relationships were part of a general rebellion against conventional systems and rules, and the truly momentous change in sexual behaviour was brought about by the advent of the birth control pill, which ushered in the so-called Sexual Revolution. Actually, young people today are not having more sex at a younger age than did the Baby Boomers (born between 1946 and 1964). Moreover, the National Health and Social Life Survey in the US reports that the use of condoms has increased among young people and hookups (casual sexual encounters) between total strangers are relatively uncommon.

However, research in the USA has shown that on-campus hook-ups between college students are quite common, engaged in particularly by people who have no desire for a long-term or committed relationship. The discourse around hook-ups is vague, contradictory and gendered. Armstrong argues that the media frequently presents hooking up as a socially accepted male behaviour, disapproved of for females, revealing the persistence of pervasive sexual double standards. When investigating tourist behaviour with regard to either phenomenon, most studies deal with cases where sex with strangers is the principal purpose of travel to the destination in question and analyse the nature of the sexual encounters involved. Several studies focus particularly on the commercial transactions and unequal power relations in sexual encounters (McKercher & Bauer, 2003).

Since our main focus here is youth tourism, the aim is not to establish a precise definition of sex in tourism, but to highlight the importance of the topic in relation to young tourists' behaviour. A recent volume on the topic edited by Carr and Berdychevsky (2022) approaches sex and tourism carefully and critically, emphasising the need to adopt a holistic approach in the study of the phenomenon and suggesting a wide-ranging perspective from which to conceptualise sex. Sex tourism entails a commercial exchange and unequal power relations between sexual partners, one of whom is often a tourist, the other a local; while sex in tourism (romance as one of the outer layer motives to travel in Pearce's (2022) travel career pattern) refers to sexual behaviour between consenting adults which does not necessarily involve a commercial transaction. The distinction between 'sex tourism' and 'sex in tourism' lies in tourists' motivations, the reciprocity (or lack thereof) and the nature of the sexual interaction. A variety of sexual activities, motivations and meaning making are involved, and Carr and Berdychevsky (2022) posit that romance among young tourists are often more spontaneous than much of the research on the phenomenon suggests, and they tend to engage in sexual activities with other tourists (rather than with locals).

In a study of young tourists' sexual activity, Eiser and Ford (1995) coin the term 'situational disinhibition' to describe the sense that a tourist may have of being a different person and feeling less responsible for their sexual escapades while away from home. Sexual behaviour among consenting young adults can be linked to their identity formation, the ways in which they build relationships and, significantly, how they conform – or not – to social stereotypes. Studies show that female tourists are willing to take sexual risks when they are looking for fun, opportunities for anonymous experimentation, and/or a sense of empowerment (Berdychevsky et al., 2013). Casual sex has, however, been found to occasionally have detrimental effects on females' psychological well-being and mental health and, particularly if such encounters take place in early adulthood, they can have long-term consequences.

A phenomenology study carried out by Berdychevsky and Gibson (2015) evidences the importance of this topic. Young female tourists recalled that it was when they were in their early adulthoods that they most often, and enthusiastically, engaged in sexual risk taking and excitement seeking while travelling/on holiday. This life stage is characterised by a sense of immortality and invincibility (Gibson & Yiannakis, 2002): young women are aware of sexual risk but feel that nothing bad or dangerous can happen to them. This sense of invincibility can be amplified on holiday, when young female tourists are more open to sexual adventure and experimentation. Referring to the geographies of engagement and encounter, Hubbard (2002) argues that sexual identities emerge from intimate interactions between self and significant other. Young fun-seeking tourists, especially females, embody the spatial and temporal fluidity of tourism experiences and tend to downplay sexual risks and prioritise fun and excitement in sexualised atmospheres. Berdychevsky (2017) argues that sexual double standards still influence gender-specific norms and that rigorous research in this field must carefully avoid any moralising or judging.

Although uninhibited sexual behaviour in tourist environments is not a new phenomenon, new risks have arisen. Little is currently known about the nexus between young adults' uninhibited sexual behaviour and their propensity to document and share photos and videos of these activities. Some young tourists film themselves or are filmed (not always with their consent) while engaging in sex. These videos are easily shared on smartphones and social network platforms or posted on pornography websites and are difficult to remove. This clearly undermines the social myth that 'What happens in Barça stays in Barça' (Harris et al., 2022). The trend requires further rigorous research and efforts have to be made to raise young tourists' awareness of such risks.

Everingham et al. (2022, p.87) have noted that

> there is little research regarding the sexual activities of youth tourists (such as, backpackers, education tourists, volunteer tourists)

more generally and this omission is particularly striking given that youth tourism is often depicted as a ritual transgression or suspension of everyday life.

The authors approach the sexual encounters of backpackers and volunteer tourists through the theoretical framework of liminality, affect and embodiment, and they suggest that some forms of tourism, for example, backpacking, are more conducive to sexual adventurousness than others. It is significant that the topic of sexual interaction/activity does not appear in the normative discourse on volunteer tourism. The authors argue that discourses around backpacker tourism are more permissive with regard to sexual encounters, while those around volunteer tourism ascribe more value to morality and altruism than to hedonistic experiences. They note that young tourists' sexual encounters are usually spontaneous and situational rather than planned in advance.

Most research on sex in tourism and youth tourist behaviour is Western-centric. In their book on young Asian tourists, Khoo-Lattimore and Yang (2018) make the point that this group's sexual behaviours and encounters are relatively under-researched. A possible reason for this may be that researchers from Asian backgrounds avoid the topic because it is not easy to gather data on such an intimate subject within still relatively conservative societies. Equally, of course, these traditional cultural and societal values still – to varying extents – influence young Asians and their attitudes to sex.

3.4. Festivals and Spaces of Heterotopia

Festivals give young tourists an opportunity to mix with like-minded people in a (temporary) *communitas* and to share 'peak' experiences in a state of collective effervescence with other festival-goers (Cohen, 2022). During the two years of the Covid-19 pandemic, most festivals and events were cancelled. When pandemic restrictions were lifted, the festival and event landscape quickly started to revive. Music, dance, cultural and sports festivals are flagship attractions in many destinations (Getz, 2008; Graburn, 1983). Festival and event tourism is centred around a carnivalesque tourism attraction, a kind of celebration, which is time-limited and place-specific and has a symbolical meaning for its attendees. Popular music festivals are renowned for their entertainment value, programme content, artist line-ups, excellent music and festival atmosphere. As 'out of the ordinary' events, music festivals can be expected to have a significant impact on individuals' psychological well-being. Festival-goers' attitudes and behaviours have been widely studied and we know that they attend events for a variety of different reasons. Many young tourists are motivated by the idea of having hedonistic experiences, escaping the everyday and social obligations, being able to forget their social status during the festival, being part of a festival-*communitas* (Wu et al., 2020). Attending a music festival with like-minded others is about both entertainment and the expression of individual taste and one's cultural consumption preferences. Festivals – 'out of the ordinary' events experienced with like-minded people – are important drivers in youth tourism.

The five festivals I explore in the next paragraphs – Coachella Valley Music, Burning Man, Midi Music Festival, Sydney Mardi Gras and Sziget Festival – are organised in 'places out of places'. Foucault (1986) argued that these self-referential spaces – heterotopias – function in relation to other spaces and are a kind of 'space of illusion', a mirrored place that present society in its perfected form. Defined by the Oxford English Dictionary Online (2022) heterotopia is

> a place (or notional place) that exists as an ordinary part of a society but which is also in some way demarcated, separate, or marginal, meaning the norms of wider society (though present) can become blurred, undermined, resisted, or transformed by different modes of thought and behaviour arising within the place itself.

The term also refers to the contestation of everyday social rules and order and involves a kind of inversion, a counter-site for transgression.

One of the biggest music festivals in the United States, the Coachella Valley Music and Arts Festival, takes place in an arid rift valley. Coachella line-ups include top names in electronic music, pop, rock and hip-hop and attract a diverse, all-age audience of about 750,000 people from all over the world. Concerts are organised on multiple stages and the festival area includes several interactive art installations. The event attracts all sorts of artists and creatives, not just musicians, to its desert location. As a novelty to celebrate the end of the Covid-19 pandemic, festival-goers were invited to enter the Coachellaverse and participate in a gamut of immersive virtual reality and geo-specific augmented reality experiences. Attendees shared their experiences on Instagram during and after the event, and even afterwards could – and still can – maintain a presence in the Coachellaverse through the Coachella Instagram profile (https://coachella.com/coachellaverse). The visual content and AR experiences shared by festival-goers on social media will, it is hoped, reinforce the festival's high reputation and foster its image as a 'must-attend' music and art festival for young people. Heterotopia juxtaposes the virtual space of the Coachellaverse, a 'space of illusion', with the festival's desert environment.

Nevada's Black Rock Desert, another arid and unhospitable setting (St John, 2018), is the location of the Burning Man Festival. This nine-day-long event, which began in 1986, has evolved from a local festival into a global, progressive, counter-cultural event (and movement) which attracts over 70,000 festival-goers (St John, 2018). Participants – known as 'Burners' – organise everything themselves because the festival does not provide any services. In recent years, Burning Man has become a benchmark festival for co-created and transformative events. Artists produce futuristic mega art installations, many of which are designed to be consumed by fire in various spectacular ways. This destruction highlights the temporary character of the event: art is born, but then disappears, into the desert. The Burning Man festival represents for many an expression of the conflict between our desire for absolute freedom and our longing to be together in community. If we accept that attending a festival can transform a person's life, and given that these events are time-limited and site-specific, environmental psychology can provide important insights into the interplay between festival-goers' psychology and behaviour and the (festival) environment. According to Neuhofer et al. (2021, p. 2), 'transformative experiences are generally described as occurrences that alter individuals' mindsets and cause immutable changes in their physical and mental states'. The festival's heterotopia, a 'city' constructed in the desert and managed by the 'Burners', is the place where transformation occurs. The festival's transformative power which, in turn, is enhanced by the physical environment – the dust, sand, heat, sunrises and sunsets, the fires – is what motivates 'Burners' to attend. In other words, the desire to lose oneself in a thought-provoking and fully immersive festival in an extraordinary setting was the principal push factor for festival-goers. The dream-like atmosphere of a heterotopia triggered their transformative experiences and self-actualisation. And these are transformations which are taking place in an arid wasteland forecast to face record periods of drought in the near future.

The Midi Music Festivals in China take place in the outskirts of overpopulated megacities – Beijing, Shanghai, Suzhou and Shenzhen. Wu et al. (2020) employed a multimethod reflexive ethnographic approach to investigate festival-goers' interactions and the meanings that they assign to such events. Longitudinal data were collected over a three-year period (2014–2017) at seven Midi Music Festivals in mainland China. These are rock music festivals, a kind of 'Chinese Woodstock' (Wu & Dai, 2018) where emerging and student bands and established Chinese rock bands play to passionate audiences. The geographical and cultural setting is particularly significant because most studies on festivals and/or young tourists' behaviour at events are set in Western countries, mainly the USA, UK and Australia. Young attendees at Midi Music Festivals, which are relatively 'alternative', reported feeling as if they were in a utopian environment where they could express their authentic selves, surrounded by friends and like-minded people. The authors discovered that the festival-goers did not simply want to escape mundanity but had been consciously planning, preparing and organising for the event to which they were deeply attached. This anticipation of the festival intensified their experiences. The festivals were experienced by attendees as collective events in which the importance of encounters, friendships and the opportunity to share beliefs and worldviews came to the fore. Midi Music Festivals, interpreted as 'temporal heterotopias' provided spaces for a – albeit temporary – peaceful and egalitarian society, one of the most significant aspects evidenced by Wu et al. (2020) in the interviews.

The Sydney Mardi Gras festival is one of the biggest Pride events in Australia (de Jong, 2017). Each year, Mardi Gras attracts hundreds of thousands of participants, mostly tourists who have fun marching alongside and admiring the satirical floats. The first Mardi Gras was organised by a handful of people back in 1978 as a protest and a demand that diversity be recognised and celebrated within an inclusive society. Many of the 1978 protesters were arrested; now, times have changed and the Sydney Mardi Gras has become an iconic event for the LGBTQIA+ community. However, many people claim that the festival has lost its original identity as a protest event and a platform for vibrant social critique and defiance of political oppression. They feel that it has been commodified and is now just a branded event mainly focused on attracting international tourists. Anne de Jong (2017) employed a feminist-embodied framework within which to analyse the encounters of one participant and thereby challenge the oversimplified but well-nigh ubiquitous narrative of the festival as a commodity. The meanings that we give to, and our understandings of, all encounters and events are subjective, situational and negotiated. De Jong's exploration – through one person's diary, reflections and photo documentation – of the commodification of Sydney's Mardi Gras is no exception. Nevertheless, this subjectivity is valuable in that it enables us to see past the many simplistic, stereotyped descriptions of the festival.

One of the biggest music, cultural and arts events in Europe takes place on the 'Island of Freedom', in Budapest (Hungary). The first Sziget Festival was in 1993, shortly after the fall of the Berlin Wall and the end of Hungary's communist era. The green island in the river Danube (*Sziget* means island in Hungarian) can only be accessed by crossing the K-Bridge. Festival-attendees live in a temporal heterotopia, camping there for a week and attending several different concerts and exhibitions (szigetfestival.com/en/). Over 60 per cent are young tourists from Germany, Italy, the Netherlands and the UK. The concerts, music line-ups, community, friendships, open-mindedness, freedom and the island's particular atmosphere have all been cited as the most important elements of the Sziget Festival. Alcohol and drug consumption are also reported to contribute to the festival's atmosphere (Michalkó, 2022; Mitev, 2007b).

A Hungarian research team (Jakab et al., 2020) have approached the study of tourists' and residents' drug consumption from a novel and interesting perspective. Budapest, the Hungarian capital, has several well-known thermal baths and spas. During the summer, many tourists frequent the spas, while residents, mostly elderly, go to them during the winter. The authors analysed the pharmaceutical contamination of untreated thermal waters discharged into the river Danube. Their study employed mass spectrometry to perform a simultaneous multi-residue drug analysis; the samples were collected pre-season, off-season and during the main tourist season. Findings show that

> the local anaesthetic drug lidocaine, antiepileptic carbamazepine, analgesic derivative tramadol and illicit drug cocaine were detected in more than half of the samples. Caffeine, metoprolol and bisoprolol (cardiovascular drugs), benzoylecgonine (cocaine metabolite), diclofenac (NSAID), citalopram (antidepressant) and certain types of hormones also have a significant frequency of 30–50%. (Jakab et al., 2020, p.399)

It was also observed that the occurrence of hormones and hallucinogenic drugs in thermal waters was high in the main tourist season, when flagship events like the Sziget Festival, mostly attended by international tourists, were taking place.

We have now visited a diverse range of places, across three continents, functioning as heterotopias. Fantasy worlds are *par excellence*, heterotopias and spaces of illusion. In the next section, youth tourism experiences linked to the fantasy world – films, TV shows, anime, manga – are addressed.

3.5. Fandom-Tourists: Film Tourists, Anime, Cosplay

All over the world, young people in our postmodern societies are crazy about pop-culture and consequently studying youth tourism in relation to entertainment is a useful exercise (Yamamura & Seaton, 2020). The content available on video-on-demand platforms such as Netflix, Amazon Prime and Disney+, combined with very extensive media coverage, feeds an almost insatiable appetite for – now readily available – information, news and gossip about celebrities, films and filming locations. Fandom tourism, pop-culture tourism, screen and film-induced tourism: all involve tourists travelling to destinations related to media personae, TV shows, movies, reality programmes and soap operas (Steinecke, 2016).

Young people are eager consumers of cultural and creative industry products and this consumption shapes their social identities. Fan-tourists travel to tourism destinations where they hope to meet an adored celebrity. Tours, products and services are organised around fandom, promoted in virtual communities and commented on and evaluated by fan-tourists (Irimiás et al., 2021). The *Harry Potter* movies and highly popular TV shows such as *Game of Thrones* have remarkably solid fanbases. Fans collect memorabilia, create virtual communities and participate in events that make them feel that they belong to the communities that evolve around films and TV shows. Tourists visit the settings of stories and film locations. Reijnders (2021) speaks about the *lieux de imagination*, the tangible, physical places of fantasy or fictive worlds, and New York is one of these as the next insight from a young tourist show (Image 2).

Fans tend to establish a psychological relationship with media personae. This kind of imagined relationship, which exists only in the mind of a fan or regular viewer, is known as a 'parasocial relationship'. TV viewers often talk to media personae they see on the screen. Regularly watching the news, the weather forecast or a specific TV programme, causes people to perceive media personae as acquaintances, people whom they come to believe they have known for a long time. Horton and Wohl (1956) called these viewer reactions to media personae 'parasocial interactions' and argued that viewers often engage in imaginary interpersonal communication with the media personae whom they see on screen. Parasocial interactions with characters in long-running TV shows, such as *Friends*, *Game of Thrones* or *Stranger Things*, for example, can lead to an imaginary dialogue with a character and cause a viewer to respond to the character's behaviour as if the latter were actually known to them. According to Cohen (2001), when audience members identify with a TV show character they can lose self-awareness and become totally immersed in a fictive situation or story. This sensation of being immersed in a story makes many viewers believe that their imaginary relationships with fictive characters are real, and this psychological merging with a particular fictive character allows the viewer to participate vicariously in that character's experiences (Schiappa et al., 2007). Viewers may laugh, cry, be worried or satisfied and feel empathy with a fictive character, and this

Image 2.   Mesmerised by New York City.
The ultimate destination for me was always New York. Just look at my face, I was this happy 24/7 when in The City! I believe that I visited during the most wonderful time of the year, at Christmas. I literally cried myself on the way from Brooklyn to Manhattan when I saw the Statue of Liberty and the skyline of the city. Still feels like it was a dream, so can't wait to return and be mesmerized again. (Courtesy by: Eszter Klapka)

identification is crucial to ensuring that they keep on watching the TV series in question (Reijnders, 2021).

Netflix is currently the world's leading streaming entertainment service with 220.67 million subscribers, the majority of whom are adults aged between 18 and 54 (Statista, 2022a). If we accept the ideas presented in the previous paragraph, the popularity of Netflix productions is evident partly due to the imaginary relationships that viewers establish with characters in the various series. Drawing on balance theory, Russell and Stern (2006) investigated the link between watching a TV show or film and purchasing spin-off products. The skyrocketing sales of merchandise related to the worlds of *Harry Potter*, *Game of Thrones* or the *Lord of the Rings*, just to mention the most popular examples, clearly evidence the extent to which watching movies and TV shows, and the parasocial relations with media personae that develop out of this watching, can influence real-life behaviour (Gyimóthy, 2018; Lovell & Thurgill, 2021).

Studies in the field of film-induced tourism have also demonstrated a link between watching films/TV shows and a wish to visit the relevant filming locations. Recently, Ryanair offered tourists a 'Netflix tour of Europe' (www.ryanair.com/try-somewhere-new) taking in Madrid, Paris and Birmingham and inspired by the Netflix productions filmed in these cities which had created alternative meanings for these locations.

3.6. Anime, Manga and Cosplay

Japanese anime and manga fandom, which began in Japan in the 1960s, is becoming an increasingly interesting area of study as these art forms' remarkably powerful influence on young people continues to grow worldwide. The Anime Industry Report (2021) shows that the most important overseas markets for anime are the USA, Canada, South Korea, Taiwan and China. The global value of the market in 2021 was 2.426 trillion yen despite the fact that the production and release of new anime was badly hit by the Covid-19 pandemic. And demand for anime productions and online games based on anime and manga is still increasing. In 2022, only 18 per cent of high-school and university students in Japan consumed this type of content on a daily basis (Statista, 2022b). In China, 64 per cent of teenagers and emerging adults (aged 13–25) said that watching animation movies was their principal leisure activity, followed by online shopping (57%), anime, comics and games (25.9%); 23.5 per cent of the youth population said travelling was their favourite activity (Statista, 2022b).

'Anime' – short for 'animation' – is a 'mass-mediated' art form, created and produced in Japan. These media productions differ significantly from Western cartoons and animated films in their production aims and meaning creation (Tung et al., 2019). Most anime TV shows and video games have been adapted from 'mangas', exquisitely drawn Japanese comic books, considered by many to be an art form in their own right.

Anime/manga tourism has become a niche-tourism market (Tung et al., 2019). The global popularity of anime led Japanese DMOs to believe that they could become a successful tourism product; the idea was that anime-fans, like film-induced tourists, would want to visit real-life locations where their favourite stories were set. Anime and manga, however, are not set in any specific place, and landscape is, in general, less relevant than in Western productions (Kirillova et al., 2019; Tung et al., 2019). The potential of anime and manga-induced tourism can only be fully realised if the study of young fans takes cultural differences – in self-expression, in spirituality and in interpersonal and intrapersonal relations – into consideration.

Anime and manga fans have been consuming and producing images and costumes for decades. Here, we define a fan as someone who is passionate about a (sub)cultural product and participates in sociocultural activities within a community made up of other fans. The previously discussed concept of *communitas* is again highly relevant in this context: young people crave to belong, to be part of a group in which they can express their thoughts and feelings and can try to be unique without being judged. Anime and manga fandom, which is based on the circulations of visuals, functions as an alternative community (Chen, 2007).

The core substance of anime and manga fandom is a visual narrative that stimulates creative imagination. The art forms' uniqueness lies in their characters – expertly and delicately drawn, with their wide eyes and brightly coloured hair – and in their extraordinary capacity to please viewers/readers and draw them deep into a fantasy world. Anime and manga often address topics and issues that are still taboo in modern Japanese society. Most fans begin to watch and read anime and manga when they are 8 or 9 years old, and comics and anime shows are their favourite media. *Attack on Titans, Evangelion, Dragon Ball* and *Fullmetal Alchemist* are among the internationally popular titles that have been part of many fans' childhoods and adolescence. Research has shown that anime/manga have a powerful influence on children and young people who are fascinated by the distinctive visuals, the symbolic meaning of the content and the teen-age characters. The fan community is closely bonded, with many fans exhibiting high levels of subcultural literacy which are greatly appreciated by their peers.

Neon Genesis Evangelion (*NGE*), created by Hideaki Anno at the Gainax studio, and broadcast in the 1990s, is one of the best examples of the high-art, experimentalism and intellectual sophistication of anime. I am going to discuss NGE in some detail, to try to dispel any reader prejudice (which I recognise in myself!) against teen/youth tastes and interests and to avoid superficial stereotyping of the anime and manga subculture. I do not believe that fandom should be considered a 'psychological symptom of a presumed social dysfunction' (Jenson, 1992, p.9).

NGE is set in a dystopian, futuristic Japan that has been rebuilt following the Second Impact that destroyed much of Planet Earth. The term Evangelion – with its religious flavour – comes from the ancient Greek for 'good news'. The main character Shinji Ikari is a problem child, recruited to drive a giant biomechanical robot (Eva) to combat the monstrous Angels (alien-like entities) that threaten to bring about an apocalypse on Earth. NGE is no simple cartoon. It is complicated and mysterious, distils a range of religious and spiritual references and even engages with Freudian psychoanalysis. Internal monologues, widely used in all anime and manga, are more common than dialogue, and the main characters often dig deep into their own psyches. NGE questions every belief, provides a path towards forgiveness and acceptance of the past and portrays an oppressive society that must be faced head on by those who want to avoid being crushed by it. It is also a coming-of-age narrative, as the story evolves the characters – and viewers – turn from *shōnen* (male adolescents) into *seinen* (adult men). Afficionados say that each scene of the 20-minute episodes needs to be viewed many times in order to really understand the enormous potential hidden within the narrative of a dystopian future.

NGE has had a clear impact on fan-tourism. Sasashima Live district in the city of Nagoya – chosen because it bears a certain resemblance to Tokyo-3, the setting of NGE – is home to a 6-metre-tall Evangelion statue, part of a tourism campaign that aims to attract fan-tourists to this newly developed district. In 2021, in order to strengthen the link between Nagoya and NGE, the city's train was renamed the Ayanami Line. The line displays the main Evangelion characters with whom fans can interact using a mobile app while travelling.

Kirillova et al. (2019) analysed the (potential) Chinese anime tourism market, exploring whether or not fans would be keen to participate in eventual tours of anime-locations. The anime-fans surveyed were aged between 16 and 30 and were active in Bilibili, one of the major online anime communities in China. Among the reasons that the survey participants gave for their fandom were a desire to blur reality and fantasy, to express social belonging and to enhance their self-development. They did not express any interest in visiting specific physical locations connected with favourite anime or in immersion in (anime) stories. Chinese anime pilgrims' social identity construction was recently analysed by Liu et al. (2021), and they found that tourist behaviours at anime sacred sites contributed to the construction of anime-tourist identities.

The Japanese fan term 'cosplay' is a portmanteau of 'costume' and 'play'. Cosplayers come together at events, known as conventions, where they engage in costumed role-play and other forms of performance art. Intensive sociocultural occasions attended by fans from all over the world, conventions have taken place in diverse cities: Bridgetown (Barbados), Kathmandu (Nepal), Los Angeles (the USA), Mannheim (Germany), Novosibirsk (Russia), Perth (Australia), San Josè (Costa Rica), Tokyo (Japan) (www.animecon.com) and, of course, Nagoya (Japan) where the World Cosplay Summit is held annually. The Anime Expo in Los Angeles welcomes around 86,000 attendees every year, half of whom are female (data on gender is no longer collected at registration, however) and a surprisingly large proportion is adults in their 40s. Most of these events are run by not-for-profit organisations and volunteers who are anime-fans and wish to give something back to the fan community.

Cosplay allows fans to actively participate and interact with like-minded people and to bring their fantasies and desires to life by dressing up and playing their favourite anime/manga characters. Playing the part of an anime character is much more than imitation. Cosplayers adapt their identity to the character, create and wear sophisticated costumes, use appropriate make up and speak in a specific jargon (Chen, 2007), and they feel that they are making their favourite anime or manga characters come to life. Fans will usually identify themselves with a character whose physique and personality are similar to their own: in their imaginations, the fact that they look like the character whom they are playing enables them in some way to share/participate in the character's inner life too. Conventions are performative expressions of anime/manga subculture and fans' motivations for attending are diverse; the most common are symbolic self-expression and finding a sense of belonging. In creating their own costumes, all cosplayers become artists contributing to the cultural wealth of the anime/manga community of festivals in heterotopia.

3.7. Conclusions

This chapter has offered a subjective overview of young tourists' hedonistic experiences. The societal changes currently influencing young adults' attitudes and behaviours, both in their everyday lives and on holiday, have been considered. The changing discourse on intimate relationships, 'situationships', challenges our understanding of young tourists and intimacy. Much research has been done on 'pleasure peripheries' where social norms can be suspended, leading to transgressive behaviour. Michel Foucault's concept of 'heterotopia' – that stands in opposition to utopias and dystopias, which are not physical, real places – presents society in a perfected form, but turned upside down. Temporal heterotopias such as seaside and ski-holidays, festivals and cosplays allow young tourists the space and time to live cathartic and extraordinary experiences and thus, crucially, the 'freedom to be'.

Chapter 4

The Young Tourist and Social Media

Human social life has always been shaped by technology and its innovations. Access to new technology and media allows like-minded people to connect and to build communities. The impact of digitalisation on young tourists' behaviour is generally recognised, and most tourism destinations and services reach out to the youth segment on social media. The tourism sector is inevitably affected – both positively and negatively – by our technology-driven society. The topic is too extensive to cover fully in this chapter where we will, instead, focus on young tourists' use of smartphones and social media while travelling/on holiday. This is justified by the documented prevalence of smartphone use by young tourists (Tussyadiah & Wang, 2016). For many, smartphones are an extension of their body, some people ascribe human characteristics to them. The perception of their smartphone as a personalised travel companion, and a substitute for real life human contacts, will almost inevitably shape a young tourist's experiences. The chapter also explores young tourists' use of travel information and the social relations they establish and maintain while travelling. Smartphones and contemporary media technology are heavily used to record, post and live-stream tourism experiences, and young tourists perform the tourist role on the various social media stages. This is one of the reasons why the young are often considered narcissistic.

4.1. Gen Me: Are Today's Youth Narcissistic?

Young people today are often accused of narcissism, self-importance and grandiosity. In the scientific literature, definitions of narcissism are myriad and by no means consistent. Extreme narcissism is pathological, but the term is also used loosely to describe an overly self-absorbed attitude. There is an ongoing debate on whether young people's self-focused attitudes should be seen positively or negatively. In social history, older adults have often considered subsequent generations to be strange, extravagant or 'offbeat' and their efforts to understand young people's behaviour have been filtered through their adult expectations of how the young *should* behave.

The Youth Tourist: Motives, Experiences and Travel Behaviour, 63–81
Copyright © 2023 by Anna Irimiás
Published under exclusive licence by Emerald Publishing Limited
doi:10.1108/978-1-80455-147-920231005

In the social sciences youth behaviour is commonly, and almost always pejoratively, described as narcissistic. The psychologist Jean Twenge (2006) has suggested that levels of narcissism vary both between generational cohorts and during the course of an individual's life. Writing in 2006, she argued that people born between 1970 and 1990 were more narcissistic than any previous generation had been (when they were young). Based on cross-generational data gathered from 1.3 million young Americans, Twenge (2006) found that the young focus almost entirely on themselves. The American college students whom she surveyed were very much focused on themselves, had low environmental and civic engagement, preferred leisure to work and commitment and sought instant gratification. In fact, her experience prompted her to coin the term 'Generation Me'. The shift in Gen Me values has speeded up over time and is predicted to continue to do so. Twenge's research seems to indicate that narcissism levels change as people grow older and tend to decrease in later life. Older people are rarely described as narcissistic in normative discourses. However, this does not mean that they are not narcissistic: most studies are carried out with young adults and do not consider seniors. Hardly any research on narcissism has involved longitudinal data gathering (Cramer, 2011). So we simply do not have the data.

Young adults, like any other population group, are extremely heterogeneous, and it is both unfair and misleading to label an entire generation as excessively narcissistic. The assumption that all youth tourists conform to the Generation Me stereotype and believe themselves to be special and more important than anyone else may bias the normative discourse on youth tourism. There has, in fact, been research that contradicts the 'Gen Me' narrative, arguing that narcissism has not actually been increasing in the last decades and providing evidence from long-term research on the behaviours of emerging adults (Paulsen et al., 2015). A healthy personality develops throughout a person's life, and by the time most people move into their 40s they are usually more self-controlled, more responsible and, hopefully, more emotionally stable than their younger selves. As adults, it may be all too easy to ignore the fact that we all change as we grow up, and that certain character developments that we imagine to be historically (externally) driven are, in fact, the result of internal factors: individuals in their 20s do not think or behave as they will in their 40s. And now, to return to narcissism and our efforts to assess it.

The Greek myth of Narcissus (Νάισσος), a hunter whose obsession with his own beauty led to his death, has inspired painters, sculptors, psychoanalysts and marketing and management experts alike. The myth warns us of the dangers of self-obsession and seeing what we want to see: an idealised self-image looking back at us from the mirror. The managerial implications provided by some studies in tourism marketing and management that have analysed tourism offers are grounded in an assumption that today's youth are, for the most part, narcissistic. Dean MacCannell (2002, p.150) argued that, from a psychoanalytic perspective, tourism is built on the 'narcissistic ego structure' and therefore travelling to commercialised tourism attractions, specifically built to entertain tourists, is a self-satisfying 'ego project'. Narcissism has been identified as the driver of youth consumer behaviour. Twenty years after MacCannell, Corbisiero (2022, p.54) described young tourists as 'narcissistic, selfish and politically disengaged'. He goes on to suggest that tourism marketing strategies should reflect tourists' narcissistic attitudes and behaviours while also finding ways to resonate with millennials' progressive mindsets. This approach, however, fails to recognise how complex 'narcissism' is and thus interprets the construct much too narrowly.

Narcissism is a psychological construct and a personality feature which can lead to both vice and virtue (Paulsen et al., 2015). The clinical theorisation of narcissism began with Sigmund Freud who said that a narcissist loves his/her own image as an object is loved by the Other. Thus, narcissism is only partially self-referential since the image becomes the object of the love, desire and interest of the meaningful Other. Psychologists distinguish between adaptive (normal, healthy) and maladaptive narcissism (psychopathology) and identify two subtypes: grandiose and vulnerable narcissism. The narcissist needs the recognition of others, while lacking any empathy for them, and has a powerful sense of entitlement. Exhibitionism and a compulsion to achieve is linked to grandiose narcissism, while vulnerable narcissism is characterised by insecurity, anxiety and a tendency to hostility. In the first decades of the twenty-first century, narcissism, heightened confidence and related personality qualities started to establish themselves within the normative discourse on (the then adolescent) Generation Z.

Social science studies assess narcissism based on scales such as the Narcissistic Personality Inventory (Ames et al., 2006) or the Hypersensitive Narcissism Scale (Hendin & Cheek, 1997). In clinical psychology, studies employ the Narcissistic Personality Disorder (NPD) scale to diagnose pathological personality disorders and anti-social behaviour. Levels of arrogance, authority, exhibitionism, exploitativeness, entitlement, empathy, self-absorption, self-admiration, superiority and vanity are assessed through these scales. These surveys are based on self-reporting and are therefore inevitably subject to a degree of bias. The NPD has also been criticised over the years because important healthy personality attributes such as self-esteem and positive self-image can sometimes be misdiagnosed as psychopathological narcissism.

In tourism, Canavan (2017) reflected on the implications of increased levels of narcissism among tourists. She argued (2017, p.1322) that tourism, because of its elements of 'exploitation, entitlement and exhibitionism', provides an ideal environment for reinforcing narcissistic traits. In Canavan's view, the normalisation of self-representation (on social media) in tourism contexts may be hindering the development of sustainable tourism. Selfies – often interpreted as epitomising excessive self-love and an exaggerated attention to the self – cannot but be associated with narcissism. And there is evidence that the contemporary phenomenon of the selfie and its sharing on social media shapes, modifies and can sometimes actually be said to determine youth tourism behaviour (Dinholp & Gretzel, 2016). For many, taking and posting a selfie with a flagship tourism attraction in the background is very probably both a completely natural and a very important part of their holiday. Selfies are defined as: 'A photograph that one has taken of oneself, *esp.* one taken with a smartphone or webcam and shared via social media' (Oxford English Dictionary Online, 2022). Christou et al. (2020) argue that some aspects of narcissism, that is, the obsession with self-presentation and

representation, are pervasive in contemporary tourism contexts. Based on structured interviews with 52 tourists (aged between 18 and 70), the authors found that
tourists – young and old – take selfies and share them via social media as a way
of enhancing their status and prestige. A selfie with an impressive landscape or
a flagship attraction behind you is interpreted as a statement of self-promotion.
The important thing is being able to feel – and proclaim – 'I've been there!' Based
on their exploratory findings, the authors argue that tourism visuals display tourists' idealised self-image and the actual tourism attraction is usually eclipsed by
the figure of the selfie-taker; the consequent 'selfie-attraction-shading effect' can
be interpreted as a manifestation of a narcissistic tourist behaviour (Christou
et al., 2020, p.292).

Some researchers have associated such selfie-taking behavioural trends with
a society in which adolescent character traits have become prevalent. Sharpley
(2021, p.439), however, has argued that while contemporary tourists play a more
proactive and performative role in their photographic practices, this should not be
confused with narcissism. The affordances of the smartphone have transformed
the practice of travel photography. Most young tourists use their smartphones to
capture and immediately share photos within their network. Significant attitudinal and behavioural changes which can convincingly be related to narcissism are
evident in contemporary society. However, we have little or no archival data on
how narcissistic young people were in the past and there are therefore no grounds
for claiming that today's youth are more narcissistic than their predecessors down
the generations. For cultural reasons, too, generalisations about narcissistic youth
tourist behaviour are misleading: no research – comparative or otherwise – has
yet been done on youth narcissism in different cultural contexts, in collectivistic
versus individualistic societies, for instance. Consider the Image 1.

4.2. Togetherness and Performing Roles

Young people's time – whether in the family, related to social obligations or planning holidays – is usually structured by adults and determined by the latter's
interests and choices. Youth tourists thus experience autonomy and freedom from
family constraints when they start organising their own holidays. Young people
often travel with groups of friends. Exploring tourism behaviour through the study
of such groups is helpful and reveals the ways in which hedonistic pleasure and
fun shape group engagement and cement allegiances. Attending sporting events
such as a Premier League football match, Formula 1 or the Moto GP, young fans
express their commitment to a particular team or person. Being immersed in a
fan-experience together gives young adults great pleasure, and sharing good times
enhances group engagement and subjective well-being. Nowadays, the fact that
these collective experiences are re-lived repeatedly through narratives strengthens social bonds. Having fun together – playing, joking around – helps to create
a sense of community and produces social cohesion, both vital to the healthy
personal development of teens and young adults.

Today, young people spend more time on social media than with friends.
Fewer opportunities for in-person social interactions deprive young adults of

Image 1.   A Selfie Taken by a Young Couple at Machu Picchu.
We set out to discover South America in a particularly important period of our life. We both agree that it was a transformative journey. Here our faces show both the fatigue and the satisfaction we felt at one of the 'Seven wonders of the modern world'. Being there taught us that we can never know enough about the incredible works of other civilisations. (*Source*: Courtesy by Edoardo Marangon and Fiamma Elena Gomez)

'collective effervescence' (Durkheim, 1912), times of shared participation that strengthen friendships and bond a community together. In the digital space boundaries between private and public, frontstage and back have been blurred by the ubiquity of information technology in our daily lives. The sociologist Erving Goffman (1959) studied social reality in face-to-face encounters. He considered human social interactions to be performances, arguing that individuals perform different roles in different situations, modifying their interactions (and behaviours) in accordance with how they and their fellow 'performers' (implicitly) agree a situation to be. This dramaturgical approach assumes that individuals have their frontstage public persona and keep their inner life backstage. On the frontstage, behaviour, appearance and communication styles are shaped by social expectations. Backstage, on the other hand, people (largely) drop their masks and interact more spontaneously within their intimate social circle. On social media 'stages', however, public and private lives overlap, intimate travel – like all other – experiences are very widely shared. Whether the act of performance is more meaningful for some young tourists than the tourism experience itself remains an open question.

4.3. Wanderlust

Wanderlust, a German word adopted into English, is a widely used term and concept in tourism, usually associated with transformative travel experiences.

However, until 1970s, a clear definition of the concept was missing from tourism literature. Gray (1970) made a distinction between *sunlust* and *wanderlust* tourism based on tourists' diverse motivations and tourism behaviours and argued that tourists experiencing wanderlust want to discover new cultures and people, while *sunlust* tourists are more passive and prioritise relaxation. Kock et al. (2018) approached 'wanderlust from a different perspective, that of evolutionary psychology, arguing that it – along with affiliation, status, mating and the need to evade harm – is one of the five shapers of tourism behaviour'. With a focus on tourist types, Sharpley (2018, p.114) argued that 'the explorer-wanderlust-allocentric tourist is typecast as being bold, adventurous, independent and empathetic to new cultures and societies'.

Investigating the word's etymology, Irimiás and Mitev (2023) reflected on the origins of the concept of 'wanderlust'; the exact German translation of the two words that make up this compound noun (*wander* = to hike and *Lust* = desire) reveal the term's origins in the German Romantic movement. In fact, the pleasure of hiking was often captured on canvas, as the artists of the time observed the natural world and its landscapes with a critical eye and tried to find within these wonders the reflection of their own inner selves. One of the masterpieces from the era is Caspar David Friedrich's 'Wanderer above the Sea of Fog' [*Der Wanderer über dem Nebelmeer*], painted in 1818. The solitary male figure is depicted from behind, and he is contemplating a range of rocky peaks emerging from the fog. This depiction of the Elbe Sandstone Mountains (in what is now the Czech Republic) was intended to evoke the sublime – the aesthetic and spiritual grandeur of nature that cannot but stimulate self-reflection. Ever since the nineteenth century hiking has been extremely popular in Germany where, each year, Hiking Day [*Tag des Wanderns*] is celebrated on 14 May, a day of hiking tours and workshops that are participated in by more than 1.5 million passionate hikers.

So, as we have touched upon, the term wanderlust originally (in the late eighteenth century) referred to the desire of (mainly) young adults to escape their often-restrictive domestic environments and explore the world (Irimiás & Mitev, 2023). In other words, wanderlust is primarily a strong desire to explore. While many tourism studies take for granted that a tourist is someone with a strong desire to travel and to explore (i.e. that s/he is motivated by wanderlust), few have actually explored the concept of desire thinking in any depth. The desire thinking that fuels wanderlust and travel craving arises from the mental images that tourists evoke about – past or future – travel experiences (Mitev & Irimiás, 2021). Although no desire to travel is – as far as we know – ever overwhelming enough to merit categorisation as addiction, the concept of desire thinking may be useful. Insights from clinical psychology can help us to better understand desire and desire thinking and may even provide a new perspective on tourism research which would allow us to capture the myriad ways in which we elaborate on thoughts and experiences. The concepts of wanderlust and travel craving can shed considerable light on the psychological aspects of travel-deprivation, experienced when an individual wishes to travel but cannot do so, whether for health, financial, economic or social reasons. Elaborating on travel thoughts, anticipating the pleasure of being on holiday/travelling and evoking travel memories are important mental processes that can alleviate the disagreeable condition of being unable to travel.

4.4. Young Tourists: The New Nomads

The vast topic of the impact of technology and digitalisation on youth travel behaviour needs to be examined in manageable units. The following section focuses on technology's role in creating a new figure, the 'digital nomad'. More than two decades ago, Makimoto and Manners (1997) predicted the phenomenon of 'digital nomads', people not confined to a workplace because they can work remotely, using information and communication technologies. In Makimoto and Manners' vision, digital technologies allow new kinds of work arrangement, and the boundaries between leisure and work, settling and travelling, thus become blurred. In contemporary society people are mobile, frequently 'on the move': digital nomads represent this mobility.

In another research, Richards (2015) refers to the new mobility paradigm and labels young tourists 'nomads', contrasting them with those who return home. The quantitative research for the study, carried out in 2012, collected 34,000 responses from young tourists. This large-scale survey was developed and distributed in collaboration with the WYSE Travel Confederation and involved 140 countries. Youth travel motivations, travel style and travel activities were assessed to explore 'nomadic behaviour'. This was a (vast) snapshot of what youth travellers were doing, the destinations they were visiting and why they were doing so. The data showed that young travellers were increasingly interested in long-haul journeys and exotic destinations. Their travel style reflected their lifestyle and identity. Richards (2015) identified the features that distinguished young tourists and defined them as backpackers, 'flashpackers' or 'global nomads'. While all young tourist categories reported high travel intensity, backpackers were found to spend an average of 77 days on the road. Flashpackers were defined as digital nomads with fluid lifestyles who stayed connected with home and their workplace while travelling and were less interested in establishing relations with locals. Global nomads were the most independent travellers, and they often tried to disconnect from other nomads and to make friends in local communities. Global nomads were more likely to use peer-to-peer accommodation services. Flashpackers accessed social media regularly. When asked about their aspirations, many young tourists said that they preferred alternating learning, working and travelling as a lifestyle rather than following the traditional life-path from studying to working to family to retirement. Richards' (2015) survey was conceptualised to investigate a particular segment of young tourists but it did not take individual personality factors and how they influence 'nomads' motives and behaviours into account.

Go Nomad (https://nomadlist.com/) is a platform on which individuals who travel to different parts of the world and work remotely share their evaluations of the destinations that they visit. Different aspects of a particular destination – living costs, internet speed, fun, safety, places to work from, walkability, etc., – are given a score from 1 to 5. People who join the 'nomad community' can exchange experiences and opinions and organise get-togethers in the city where they are staying (stays generally range from one to six months).

Mobile lifestyle practices are receiving increasing academic attention. Hermann and Paris (2020) investigated digital nomadism and the changes in leisure and work that occurred due to the Covid-19 pandemic. 'Digital nomads' are individuals who can fulfil work commitments from anywhere that can provide a good internet connection. Blatt and Gallagher (2013) wrote about 'the rise of the mobilocracy'. Richards (2015) noted this phenomenon and, as we have just seen, coined the term 'flashpackers'. In 2020–2021 the Covid-19 pandemic disrupted working modalities; under lockdown we discovered that office work did not have to be carried out at the office and that remote working was, in fact, usually efficient. The ubiquity of digital services and the adoption of technologies in workflows (online meetings and lectures, digital signatures, cloud services, etc.) made remote working a reality for many. Hermann and Paris (2020) explored the interplay between technology which allows people to be mobile and thus (in theory!) independent. They looked at some examples of countries (e.g. Estonia, Georgia and Barbados) that have focused on attracting location-independent people working remotely and therefore not physically tied to their workplace. These countries have started to issue a new type of 'digital nomad' visa, valid for up to one year. A growing number of people value the balance between work and leisure time that the digital nomad can enjoy. Their choice of destination does not have to depend on local work opportunities. Studies forecast an increase in the number of long-term remote workers globally; currently most digital nomads are still from the Global North.

4.5. Vanlife

'Vanlife' is about freedom from conventional work and the opportunity to travel while continuing to enjoy modern perks of life such as digital connectivity, online presence and entertainment. The hashtag #vanlife was invented in 2012 when Foster Huntington, a photographer and designer in his 20s, quit his job in New York City, bought a Volkswagen Transporter (VW) – which became his home for three years – and travelled across the USA, Canada and Mexico sharing photos of his 'vanlife'. The Instagram images were so captivating that thousands of young people followed his example. Many purchased a van, transformed it into a #homeonwheels, packed up their lives and started out on their own road adventure, #vanlifetravel. There are currently 13 million #vanlife Instagram posts. Within this virtual community young people share their travel experiences and tips on how to transform a van into a trendy, comfortable 'vandwelling'. Since 2012, Huntington has published two popular books, *Van Life: Your Home on the Road* (2017) and *Off Grid Life: Your Ideal Home in the Middle of Nowhere* (2020), in which he challenges the values of consumer society and strongly critiques big tech companies for shaping people's behaviour through algorithms.

When the word 'van' first appeared in American English it meant a canvas-covered horse-drawn carriage. With the advent of motorised transport, the word's meaning changed. Nowadays, a van is a light truck, a roomy, medium-sized vehicle with no side windows. The precursor of today's vanlife is the Californian surf-subculture of the 1950s when groups of young people travelled by van along the coast between San Francisco and Los Angeles and used to drive their vehicles onto the beaches, where they would then stay for short periods of time. (Ordinary cars were not used because they were not big enough to accommodate surf- and longboards.) The 1960s were the golden years for VW vans, the black-nosed yellow vehicles became the symbol of an attitude, a lifestyle, freedom and the unconventional. VW vans were also closely associated with the hippie movement and Route 66. In the 1970s, festival-goers, musicians, creatives and anti-war protesters all used VW vans, popular, too, because they were relatively cheap and could carry a lot of people. Today, vanlife is associated with a cosmopolitan movement and a minimalist lifestyle – the very limited storage space in a van forces people to make conscious decisions about their real needs. Following the Covid-19 pandemic, during which young tourists craved travel and freedom from restrictions, vanlife has become even more popular. In fact, embarking on an adventurous vanlife is high on the bucket list of many young people for whom it seems to be an ideal expression of wanderlust: leaving the beaten track, avoiding mass tourist destinations, having the chance to go on an inner (as well as outer) journey and to reflect on one's life goals.

Gretzel and Hardy (2019) have explored digital nomadism and the increasingly popular phenomenon of #vanlife from a tourism perspective. Vanlife, as we have seen, is a lifestyle characterised by minimalism. It differs from the traditional (tent) camping or campervan trip. Young people (usually in couples) transform their van into a home; most van owners give their vans a complete makeover. They pay attention to detail and personalised solutions. Vanlifers share their experiences on social media within virtual communities. They refer to 'vanlife' as a project and lifestyle, and some vanlifers report having travelled around for a couple of years. According to Gretzel and Hardy (2019), vanlifers prefer digital sociality to real-world relationships formed in campsites/around the campfire. The authors link vanlife and digital nomadism because vanlifers work while travelling and create mobile 'home-like' spaces. Devices such as film projectors and tablets are often visible in the images shared on Instagram with the hashtag #vanlife. A good internet connection, a projector and Netflix seem to be essential for #vanlife. Images shared with this hashtag almost always show the van and its dwellers immersed in the surrounding landscape, thus emphasising contact with nature, which is associated with freedom and mindfulness.

Note, however, that Instagram images do not usually depict the difficulties of vanlife. Vanlifers have to deal with practical issues such as where they can safely and legally park their van (at night, in particular). They need to be practical, good at problem solving and able to carry out basic vehicle maintenance and repairs. And living in such a small space, especially if the van is both home and workplace, can be challenging.

4.6. A Trusted Travel Companion: The Smartphone

Smartphones' functional benefits and ubiquitous connectivity have received much academic attention in the tourism literature (Magasic & Gretzel, 2020; Skinner et al., 2018). Most studies welcome all ICT as beneficial, and many of them provide managerial implications regarding how these technologies can best be exploited to influence or modify – nudge – tourist behaviour. The benefits of smartphone use in tourism – communication efficiency; immediate availability of information, booking and purchasing services; the ability to share tourism visuals on social networks – have been extensively documented.

Smartphones and social media currently dominate youth travel experiences and leisure activities. For many young people, being 'offline' is tantamount to being asleep. Connectivity and the ubiquity of the internet have produced a new phenomenon: 'iTime'. In iTime the boundaries between work and leisure, day and night, free and scheduled time are blurred (Agger, 2011). A diary study on the aggregated roles of the smartphone in leisure has revealed its dominance and the ways in which it has transformed everyday life, leisure, education and work (Irimiás et al., 2021). In this exploratory research, 52 young adults (aged 20–22) were asked to write a diary about their daily activities and the role that they attributed to their smartphone and to register their actual screentime. It was found that not only have smartphones become like extensions of most young people's bodies (the screentimes recorded showed that participants were inseparable from their phone for 9–12 hours each day) but they perceived their phone as a companion, an enabler and a separator. Participants reported that their smartphones were influencing their subjective well-being, moods and feeling. Constantly dividing their attention between online and offline activities, continuously interrupted by notifications, repeatedly scrolling social media just to check what others are up to – all of this caused participants to feel as though they were in a hybrid space/time dimension. Participants lamented their increased propensity to procrastinate and to waste time online, checking social media or watching YouTube videos, spending hours disconnected from their surroundings. On the plus side, they mentioned that the smartphone provided entertainment and enabled them to communicate with friends and stay up-to-date. In concluding this diary-keeping exercise, over half of the participants acknowledged that they needed to find a healthy balance between their online and offline leisure activities, but said that they found it extremely difficult to put their smartphones down.

These findings can also be extended to the context of tourism: when a tourist's attention is constantly returning to their smartphone screen, their capacity to immerse themselves in their tourism experience is severely compromised. In fact, tourists have been categorised on the basis of their degree of immersion in the digital world (Fan et al., 2019). While the researchers started from the premise that every tourist has a smartphone, they distinguished individual tourists according to how attached/detached they were from the digital world while travelling, categorising them as social media addicts, daily life controllers, dual zone travellers, diversionary travellers, digital detox travellers or disconnected immersive travellers.

Young tourists use different sources of tourism information. Prior to the advent of the internet of things – and before that the internet itself – tourism information flows were generated (and controlled) by service providers and destination marketing organisations; communications between businesses and tourists via marketing channels and word of mouth among friends and relatives also played very significant roles in influencing travel choices. All of these modalities have radically changed. Wang and Fesenmaier (2013) identified the different uses of smartphones in tourism information searches and also pointed to the phones' multiple other functions. A sense of connectedness was one of the most significant benefits reported by tourists.

Tourists not only 'consume' but also 'produce' information. Young tourists produce most of the content that they upload and share with other web-users; people who generate content and share travel information on social media are often called 'prosumers' (Sigala et al., 2012). Many young tourists share visuals on social media to display their holiday experiences; Instagram is one of the most popular apps used to this end (Volo & Irimiás, 2021). Young tourists share their experiences of services, businesses and destinations on the dominant social media networks and rarely rely on traditional information sources such as brochures or television ads. Youth tourism experiences are undoubtedly influenced by social media. Youth tourists' pre-trip, on-site and post-trip use of social media has been documented in the literature (e.g. Tan & Yang, 2021).

4.7. Smartphones as Travel Companions

There is a tendency for young tourists to anthropomorphise their smartphones, treating them as companions and communicating with them. Anthropomorphism is the attribution of a personality and human characteristics to objects or inanimate entities. When someone sees a device as having a personality, their relationship with it is strengthened. People often identify themselves with the objects they own. A smartphone may be perceived as an extension of the self (Belk, 2018). There is no scientifically supported evidence that young tourists are more likely than older adults to use smartphone assistants or to anthropomorphise their smartphones and tourists of all ages use technological devices and apps while travelling. Their trusted travel companion immediately responds to requests, never delays and solves all sorts of problems. Tourists' affective attachment to their smartphones emerges as a key element of their tourism behaviour (Tussyadiah & Wang, 2016).

Young tourists' attitudes to proactive smartphone systems and their responses to push recommendations (nudges intended to modify human behaviour) have been found to (largely) determine their tourism behaviour (Tussyadiah & Wang, 2016). The authors (2016, p.495) consider smartphones to be 'intentional systems'; this refers to the concept of 'socially intelligent agents' that help people to make decisions. Using the 'intentional system' built into smartphones, people are trusting the device to orient them in unfamiliar environments; they ask its advice about where to eat, sleep, play and find entertainment: communicating with their phone screens, they don't think to look around them – whether for information or just to enjoy the scenery. There is no need to talk directly to service providers, taxi drivers, pedestrians or locals. Since smartphones are so central to most young adults' lives, Tussyadiah and Wang (2016) selected students to explore the phenomenon of humans' trust in their smartphones and acceptance of being 'nudged' by their devices. Participants who accepted push recommendations and changed their intended behaviour reported feeling that their smartphones were trusted travel companions. Repeated nudging, however, made many of them anxious: it was believed that 'overtrusting' a device and being too reliant on its guidance was negative.

Boundaries between experiences lived in the digital realm and in real life are blurred. Digitalisation permeates every aspect of human life and is increasingly part of all tourism experiences. Trivial experiences such as having breakfast or going for a walk while on holiday become performative acts on the social media stage. The 'post it, or it didn't happen' attitude is common among young tourists. Intentional systems are designed to display social characteristics in order to build and consolidate trust and increase user engagement. Smartphones and digital assistants are often treated like travel companions because they act like humans (giving advice and warnings, responding to queries, etc.). This trust in their devices and their relationships with 'intelligent agents' shapes tourists' behaviour, reducing their spontaneous interactions and the serendipity that used to be inherent in travel.

4.8. Nudging

Nudging can alter tourism behaviour. Indeed, it plays a key role in digitally manipulated tourism behaviour and thus deserves closer examination. The behavioural economists Richard Thaler and Cass Sunstein (2009) believe that human thinking is flawed and that this leads to irrational choices. They argue that 'nudges' can modify behaviour and lead to outcomes that align with people's real interest. The authors define a nudge as 'any aspect of a *choice architecture* that alters people's behaviour in a predictable way without forbidding any options or significantly changing their economic incentives' (Thaler & Sunstein, 2009, p.x). Nudging was first introduced into the public sphere to help people to make the right choices for their own benefit. For example, to help people to eat more healthily, choice architects displayed fresh salad in front of doughnuts in a cafeteria, thereby nudging people to make the healthier choice, even if they had originally intended to buy a doughnut. However, the marketing potential of nudging was soon recognised, as we can see all around us.

Shoshana Zuboff's (2019) *The Age of Surveillance Capitalism* provides incredibly detailed and chilling explanations of the capacity that digital and tech companies have to nudge users – through carefully designed and undetectable onscreen cues – into modifying their behaviour. The ubiquity of digital technologies means that a significant proportion of our decision-making is done in the digital environment, through a screen. Digital nudging is widely used in tourism, as the range and quantity of available apps that suggest what to do, where to go and what to buy evidences. In this context, Instagram is one of the most influential shapers of tourism behaviour (Volo & Irimiás, 2021). Social norms, too, play a significant part in guiding people's behaviour. We are continuously influenced by the decisions of others, whether in real life or on social media. Indeed, Thaler and Sunstein (2009) showed that nudging via social influence is one of the most effective ways of modifying our attitudes and behaviours.

4.9. Instagram and Influencers

Through social media, people exchange opinions with family members, friends or colleagues on the most diverse subjects such as food, fashion, entertainment or travel. Very soon after Instagram was first launched (in 2010), Xiang and Gretzel (2010) were able to demonstrate that people can establish social bonds and interact with others on social media, even when they are physically apart. Even before the advent of Instagram, young adults were spending long hours on social media platforms, following other people's activities and exchanging ideas with them (Gretzel & Yoo, 2008). A survey conducted by the Pew Research Center in 2021 found that 95 per cent of interviewed teens (n = 1,316, aged between 13 and 17) visited YouTube at least once a day and 19 per cent constantly visited the platform. According to another survey, 25.7 per cent of US Instagram users were aged between 25 and 35 years. As 'social' spaces, online platforms enable users to create and share their own content and to feel part of a virtual community.

Indeed, photos, stories, videos and live-streaming events shared on it have considerable persuasive power (Volo & Irimiás, 2021). Viewing other people's hedonistic experiences very evidently influences young tourists' consumption choices. When tourists post a travel-related image they are seeking recognition from other users (Liu et al., 2019). Heart icons and positive comments are external rewards that add prestige and glamour to their trip. Unexplored and hidden places – if they are 'Instagrammable' – are in high demand as backgrounds/settings for selfies and live-streaming videos. Diehl and Zauberman (2022) argue that online photography apps, such as Instagram, allow customisation and post-processing effects; still people need to be mindful in taking photos to enjoy the moment. The app can almost be said to provide an endless cat walk upon which to perform multiple identities. Luxury travel and its 'Intsagrammability' lie at the heart of the 'Rich Kids of Instagram' (#RKOI) phenomenon; the platform serves as a stage for extremely wealthy young people to flaunt their jet-setting luxurious lifestyles and consumption patterns. Cohen et al. (2022) showed that 'rich kids' Instagram posts, photos and IG videos of luxury travel and modes of transport (private jets, top-of-the-range cars) epitomise the lifestyles and holidays that some – though not all – of their contemporaries long for. The authors, adopting the perspective of evolutionary psychology, argued that conspicuous consumption – luxury travel and the display of 'positional goods', for instance – is among the strongest markers of power, wealth and social status in contemporary society. Instagram offers the ideal platform for displaying one's conspicuous consumption and strengthening the 'value communication' of the hyper-wealthy.

Adolescence and young adulthood are frequently associated with a propensity to take risks, challenge social taboos and seek pleasure above all else. In the tourism context, it is important to try to understand the ways in which young tourists take – or avoid – risks and thus do – or do not – get involved in hazardous situations. Young adults' risk-related behaviour, travel risk perceptions and perceptions of life-threatening events when on holiday are serious issues (Sarman et al., 2016). Travel-related risks at the macrolevel can be terrorist attacks, natural catastrophes, political insurrection and epidemics, while on a personal level risk can range from physical risks such as injuries or even death to dangerous (micro) situations. In a choice experiment survey Sarman et al. (2016) developed 12 scenarios and asked 298 young adults to evaluate how risky they perceived the different scenarios, and thus destinations, to be. Results showed that, in general, these young adults' risk perception was quite low.

Selfie-taking can also involve (sometimes considerable) risk. A systematic review of young adults' behaviour when taking selfies revealed the extent and nature of the risks associated with dangerous self-photography (Weiler et al., 2021). Instagram is the preferred platform for displaying impressive travel photos. To catch the user's attention and make them pause their scrolling, even for a few seconds, the self-photographer often feels that they need to do something eye-catching and thus potentially risky. In extreme cases, this risk-seeking behaviour can lead to severe injury or even death. Rooftops, skyscraper edges, wild animal reserves, cliffs, waterfalls or volcano edges have been the scenes of fatal selfies, known as 'killfies'. Wildlife photography and extreme sports are also potentially hazardous. The rising number of fatalities among young tourists can probably be explained by their low risk-awareness in unfamiliar surroundings and/or weather conditions. More young tourists die in India than anywhere else: taking selfies, in train accidents, mauled by wild animals or falling from heights. Weiler et al. (2021) have reported on the extent and nature of hazardous selfie-taking tourist behaviour. Although their systematic review does not specifically mention youth tourists as more likely to take risks while selfie-taking, the Eurispes Italy Report published in 2019 reported the deaths of 259 tourists while engaged in risky photograph-taking, 70.3 per cent of whom were aged between 10 and 29. This sad phenomenon calls for specific destination managerial initiatives to prevent incidents and fatalities.

4.10. Influencer Marketing

Influencers, the 'new-era prosumers', use their persuasive power to modify their followers' attitudes and behaviours and are usually trusted by a high number of followers (Gretzel, 2018; Sigala et al., 2012). They are media personae who share content on social media platforms and manage a pool of followers and whose knowledge/expertise/opinions about certain topics and/or products are trusted by their followers. Before influencers came on the scene, celebrities were used to promote products and services – through direct advertising, product placement – to a wide consumer public.

Millions of users scroll social media content to find inspiration about music, lifestyle, food, fitness and travel and influencer marketing – based on the power of social influence – has become one of the most common forms of online marketing. An individual's social influence corresponds to their ability to impact the opinions, attitudes and behaviours of others (Liu, 2019). The more trustworthy an influencer is, the more effective the advertising. In 2020, there were over 6 million brand-sponsored influencer posts on Instagram, the leading platform for influencer marketing worldwide, followed by YouTube and TikTok.

Young adults prefer social media content and e-WOM to traditional advertising because the content shared by users and/or influencers is considered more credible and trustworthy than institutional messages or brand marketing contents (Ge & Gretzel, 2018; Volo, 2021). Credibility and trustworthiness, in this context, refer to the reliability and honesty attributed to an opinion leader who showcases her/his expertise in a specific field. Baby boomers and older generations are much less likely than young adults to follow influencers.

Influencers first have to build and then maintain their visibility on social media. Their Instagram accounts show them to be accessible to their followers, often responding to the latter's comments. This perceived authenticity can lead followers to establish a psychological bond with influencers. Followers who constantly check an influencer's social media profile become entangled in consumer experiences and identify themselves through purchase/consumption and the objects that they own (Belk, 2018).

4.11. FOMO, JOMO and the metaverse

The recently defined emotions FOMO (Fear Of Missing Out) and JOMO (Joy Of Missing Out) are often exacerbated by social media use. In this section, the feelings aroused by consuming social media content are discussed. Young tourists often post and share visuals depicting their tourism experiences; these are almost always positive – memorable, rewarding, (perceived as) unique. The problem is that watching others enjoying themselves – whether sightseeing, fine-dining or having fun in some glamorous spot – can provoke envy, frustration or anxiety. FOMO is a fast-emerging topic in consumer psychology and popular media, where it is understood in terms of young people's anxiety about being left out. Social media content is designed to capture and keep users' attention for as long as possible; to do so, content is personalised and it is very often designed to make people feel insecure and vulnerable. FOMO-inducing content is everywhere on social media, and over 65 per cent of young Americans (aged between 16 and 23) reported experiencing FOMO while scrolling social media (Harris Poll, 2021).

The FOMO on something important in life and feeling regret and anxiety about this is widespread among young social media users. FOMO is commonly associated with a constant desire to check social media apps. The core psychological need for social connection is primordial, and the quality of our human contacts impacts our health and subjective well-being: well-connected individuals are healthier than those with few social contacts (Holt-Lunstad, 2022). Many young adults today spend a significant proportion of their social lives on social media, subject to a constant flow of information about other people's lives. Of course, older adults also use social media, but they still have memories of chatting with friends without immediately posting the occasion for all to witness. Mental health issues, such as depression and anxiety, are ever more common amongst young people in OECD countries. The sudden growth of this negative trend can be traced back to 2010, when social media networks began increasingly to penetrate the lives of the young (Twenge & Hamilton, 2022).

While people's identities and status are still unstable, their mood and subjective well-being are particularly vulnerable to fears about missing out on/being left out of whatever other people are doing: the pressure to be part of a community (and therefore constantly online) is felt acutely. A survey carried out during the Covid-19 pandemic among Italian and Hungarian university students explored young adults' travel craving and FOMO (Mitev & Irimiás, 2021). Participants said that they were finding social media less frustrating and reported that – because everyone was stuck at home during the lockdowns, unable to travel – they were at last free of that terrible feeling that other people were having rewarding experiences which they themselves were excluded from.

Shortly after the lockdowns were lifted, students could again leave home to participate in study abroad programmes. An auto-ethnographic study by a young female college student is presented here as an example of the complexity of FOMO as experienced during this trip. The research was carried out in the first half of 2022. Zsófi (aged 22) was an Erasmus student in Florence (Italy) for six months. She kept a diary about her social media usage and her FOMO over a period of some days.

> I looked at my phone for the first time at 9:00 a.m., right after waking up. None of my friends had posted anything in the morning, but there were still pictures and videos from last night I haven't seen yet. Pictures of sightseeing and evening walks were uploaded, which specifically did not create strong FOMO in me. I felt a slight envy of how good it was for them, but this feeling was not so strong, since I had recently returned home from vacation and my experiences were still fresh. The Instagram stories appearing two hours later caused a very strong feeling of FOMO in me. With stomach cramps and the feeling of being left out, I was attending a lecture but I was watching the van-videos, the shots taken in Venice and a breakfast video. The next time I looked at my smartphone, I was still at the University and a selfie of a Czech friend of mine with other friends made me very sad. I wanted to be there with them. At three p.m., I was writing my assignments and studying when I saw the Instagram posts of my friends jumping into the turquoise sea and eating Spanish tapas. At that point, my FOMO feeling was not that strong, I thought that it would be nice to swim in the sea, where I had been a long time ago. After that, I checked Instagram at nine p.m. but I didn't feel left out of anything because my friends were shopping and drinking Aperol Spritz, which I can do at any time. I went out to eat an Italian ice cream. I checked the Instagram posts again while I was watching a movie and again before going to bed. I saw posts about a sunset and night walks, and I was a little jealous of the wonderful time my friends had, but luckily, the ice cream I ate made up for it all.
> *Source*: Courtesy by Zsófi Szabó from her Bachelor's dissertation (2022).

Walking With Smartphone (First Weeks of Stay)	Walking Without Smartphone (Last Weeks of Stay)
• Following Google maps on my phone • Chatting with friends at home • Listening to music • Reading shop opening hours • Reading reviews of cafes and restaurants on Google • Taking pictures • Planning the route • Adding places to a list • Urge to look at my phone • Holding my phone	• Paying attention to scents and smells • Observing locals • Observing the façades of shops and buildings • Knowing the route by heart • Thinking, reflecting • Imprinting places in the mind • Capturing small moments • Nostalgia

Source: Courtesy by Zsófi Szabó from her Bachelor's dissertation (2022).

She also compared her impressions and feelings while walking in Florence with and without her smartphone, as she started to explore the city as a tourist.

These extracts from Zsófi's diary vividly illustrate how FOMO can actually cause physical pain, in this case *stomach cramps*. On the other hand, the positive outcomes of restricting social media use while travelling are also recognised by Zsófi usually: paying more attention to travel companions, being more fully immersed in immediate experiences, being in a better mood and experiencing emotional well-being. JOMO is the opposite of FOMO, and it refers to a more conscious use and engagement with social media. JOMO also refers to the freedom of unplugging and disconnection, enjoying the present moment and experiencing one's journey mindfully.

Young tourists are 'prosumers', when they post their experiences on social media they become YouTubers, TikTokers, Instagrammers and live-streamers, depending on where and what they post. Habitual excessive social media use produces negative outcomes, but greater awareness of eventual negative consequences can potentially lead to a more conscious use of social media when travelling. Choosing to avoid social media when on holiday indicates a wish to stay unplugged for a while and to enjoy a kind of digital detox. However, developments in digital technology and its tourism marketing implications seem to be leading to ever more frequent device use, with a current focus on engaging young tourists in immersive digital experiences.

4.12. Metaverse

The metaverse is conceived as a fully realised virtual universe ('meta' and 'universe'). The term was used by novelist Neal Stephenson (1992) in *Snow Crash* to describe a virtual space where people could escape their mundane world. In tourism, it refers to travel experiences lived in a blended (physical and digital) reality (Buhalis & Karatay, 2022). Virtual reality headsets and a superfast internet connection are needed to access the metaverse. As Sigala (2022, p.30 in Dwivedi et al., 2022) highlights,

> it is not the same as current immersive technologies. The metaverse is a network of always-on three-dimensional virtual environments (e.g. a combination of immersive VR, online multiplayer games and a 3D internet) in which the users interact with one another, software agents and digital objects while operating virtual representations of themselves called avatars and by using the metaphor of the real world but without its physical limitations.

Here, my aim is to provide readers with just a few insights into the metaverse and young tourists (for a comprehensive analysis of the challenges and opportunities of the metaverse see Dwivedi et al. (2022)).

Teens and young adults constitute the main target market for businesses in the metaverse. Young people accustomed to a blended life and to switching between online and offline experiences more readily engage with the metaverse and immerse themselves in a digital second life than do older individuals. Teenagers and emerging adults who have grown up with ubiquitous connectivity are skilful in their use of smart and digitally advanced products and services. Companies recommend that children under age 13 should not use the VR headsets or access the metaverse, however. As a *New York Times* reporter has warned, far too many children and teens are already spending far too much time in the metaverse (Hill, 2022). Khoo et al. (2022, p.1), conceptualising metaverse tourism and comparing its attributes to e-tourism and smart tourism, argued that 'metaverse tourism is a collection of articulate objects, humans and avatars, interfaces, and networking capabilities in the tourism industry'.

Metaverse tourism promises novel experiences in a mirror world. Both Buhalis and Karatay (2022) and Sigala (2022) in the opinion paper by Dwivedi et al. (2022) argue that travel simulations can make an intangible tourism experience tangible, and potential tourists can immerse themselves (virtually) in a destination before deciding whether to visit it in real life or not. Disneyland, for example, created its own theme-park metaverse headsetless experience with projecting customised 3D imagery of Disney characters and in the meantime Disneyland tracks visitors' movements to nudge them. Playing the racing game *Miami Street* on the virtual streets of Miami teaches players the topography of the city, useful knowledge if one ever visits it in real life. Players/potential tourists can decide on their ideal-fictive identity when selecting an avatar identity. The avatars mimic human body language, voice and gestures which makes metaverse experiences feel more like real life and thus more immersive. Most online entertainment services, especially videogames, already offer such immersive experiences, the metaverse, as Hill (2022) observed, 'is where gamers go to chill out, like skiers at an après-ski bar'.

The metaverse uses ambient intelligence which is built on pervasive computing, human profiling and context awareness. Algorithms recognise an individual's personality and emotions and the situational context. Based on the constant surveillance of users' behaviours and emotional states pervasive technologies are adaptive and personalised and can therefore modify user behaviour (Zuboff, 2019). Largely ignoring privacy concerns, the makers of Pokèmon Go, one of the most popular augmented reality games ever, were able to heavily manipulate user behaviour based on the data provided through the 'game's' avatar customisation. Gamification experiences offered in diverse tourism contexts aim to engage and please young tourists; the more personalised the game is, the more engaging it becomes.

While the metaverse tourism market is being driven by the constant extension of internet penetration, the Internet of Bodies, 5G and recently 6G availability and consumer demand for augmented and virtual reality experiences, it has still not gone mainstream. This is partly because the metaverse is proving very expensive to develop. It may also be the case that young adults are starting to tire of the ubiquity of the digital world and are sometimes choosing to spend time enjoying the real world, or even their own, undistracted, minds. Future research will have to investigate whether metaverse tourism experiences and gamification contribute to personal development, self-reflection and becoming fully adult. And do these algorithm-led virtual and digital worlds really allow individuals to have – fulfilling, pleasurable – inner (tourism) experiences?

4.13. Conclusion

The interconnectedness between young tourists' experiences and social media has received a remarkable degree of attention in academia. Chapter 4 began with an explorative discourse on narcissism. Young tourists are often described as narcissistic. Reflecting on what narcissism is and whether young adults are more or less narcissistic than older people enables us to approach selfie-taking more critically. Mainstream literature in the field of tourism shows that ubiquitous connectivity, smartphones and social media play a key role in young tourists' experiences. Posting travel images on social media is rewarding for young tourists, but in the case of 'rich kids' is very clearly an ostentation. Travel photos manifest tourists' desire for novelty and excitement, and also showing off, but the practice of selfie-taking can be risky. The original insights from young tourists presented in this chapter provide a more nuanced understanding of the role of social media in tourism.

Conclusion and Future Research Paths

This volume is a reference text principally aimed at the academic market. It builds upon a multidisciplinary literature on the young and adopts an international approach. It is designed to address the evolving nature of young tourists' motivations, experiences and travel behaviour. While the book focuses on young tourists, some connected tourism products are also discussed. Young tourists are important consumers of education, festival, fandom, film, sport and even religious tourism. These tourism products are associated with a variety of subcultures and offer young tourists enriching opportunities to build *communitas*, a sense of personal and collective identity. Youth tourism is very much about people's first unsupervised travel experiences. Historically, travelling alone or with one's peers has given the young an opportunity to awaken their sense of discovery, make their own choices and experience the joys of serendipity. Today, young tourists are virtually connected to multiple environments simultaneously, and their choices are also influenced by eWoM, nudges and push recommendations on their smartphones. More research is needed in this direction to explore the extents to which young tourists feel supported, overwhelmed or a mixture of both by the tourism service providers that harvest real-time data – on where they are, with whom, for how long and doing what – to push them towards customised services.

Young people's tourism experiences are formative and – usually – fun, and they increase adolescents' and emerging adults' social and cultural capital. While these experiences are as diverse as the young themselves, many commonalities are apparent: gaining experience as a traveller; feeling happy about successful holidays, sensing the possibility of widening one's social network, learning something new, living once-in-a-life-time experiences and capturing images to post on social media. In Pearce's (2022, p. 176) travel career pattern, the desire to raise social status at home is seen as an 'outer layer motive'. While going on fashionable holidays is often leveraged to project an image congruent with an individual's desired social status, to what extent can this be said to have become a core motivation? Some years before the era of social media, Richards and Wilson (2004, p. 43) suggested that 'the main benefit gained by students from travel was a thirst for more travel, implying that once students start travelling, they find it difficult to stop'. This 'thirst for more travel' has been intensified by the images and videos posted and shared on social media platforms, those vast new stages upon which the tourist role can be performed to perfection. The common young tourist attitude to travelling ('When, if not now?') reveals their generation-specific understanding of

The Youth Tourist: Motives, Experiences and Travel Behaviour, 83–87
Copyright © 2023 by Anna Irimiás
Published under exclusive licence by Emerald Publishing Limited
doi:10.1108/978-1-80455-147-920231006

time. As we all know, psychological time and objectively measurable 'clock' time are very different. Since its perception is both subjective and relative, the older we get the faster time seems to pass (Bejan, 2019). Most young tourists seek to experience more than one object/activity at a time. Migacz and Petrick (2018, p. 23) showed that young (millennial) tourists enjoy exploration, novelty, hedonistic experiences as much as 'being able to relax and decompress'. The motivations of well-travelled young tourists differ from those of less-experienced travellers (Pearce, 2022). But if individuals do not have the time, energy or inclination to reflect on past tourism experiences, these are unlikely to contribute to self-enhancement and self-actualisation. Self-enhancement and self-actualisation are believed to be young tourists' drivers to travel more (and responsibly).

Youth tourism, as discussed, is impacted by the prevailing socioeconomic conditions. Societal and demographic changes – like delayed life-changing events – influence young people's tourism motivations and behaviour. Many young are keen to achieve a work–life balance that includes travel, value alignment and fair pay and are prepared to switch careers to attain these goals (as the Great Resignation has shown). Digital nomads are, in part, motivated by their desire to find a satisfying work–life balance. Ubiquitous connectivity and the digitalisation of services and communication have revolutionised the ways in which young people think about learning, working and travelling (Magasic & Gretzel, 2020). Staying longer in tertiary education, for example, allows young people to use student cards and discounts (e.g. one-way student flights and interrail tickets) when travelling. Low-cost travel and the huge variety of available accommodation structures mean that travel has steadily become more accessible in recent decades, and the number of youth-oriented travel organisations and services is increasing. However, the ripple effects of the Covid-19 pandemic and the current global economic and environmental crises may very possibly slow this trend in the short-to-medium term.

The first contribution of this volume – focused upon in Chapter 1 – is its careful consideration of the social construct of 'youth/young people' and how it has evolved in relation to tourism. The generational labels used in tourism literature are also discussed. While this categorisation can help to define target segments, it can also limit/distort research since it relies too much on the classic tourism labelling of people according to age, class or income. To answer the question 'What differentiates youth tourism from other tourist segments?' young tourists' – very diverse – behaviours have been subjected to a critical analysis and compared with those of older tourists.

The second contribution of this volume is its conceptualisation of a framework for examining the interconnectedness of identity formation and tourism. Chapter 2 investigates the sphere of education-based international travel in which formal and informal learning opportunities shape young tourists' identities. The personal development dimension of identity formation is explored, with a focus on intercultural sensitivity as a competence. This perspective is based on substantive research. Work-travel, volunteer and backpacker tourism are all formative phenomena (Martins & Costa, 2022).

As young tourists have different motivations and needs, they seek pleasure and fun in diverse ways and settings. In Chapter 3, I consider young tourists' leisure activities and behaviour with a focus on selected tourism products. My findings on different social practices (festivals, entertainment) highlight young tourists' desire for group cohesion, belonging and bonding. Young people's everyday leisure activities (e.g. consuming anime and manga, films and TV shows) have been found to shape their travel intentions and tourism behaviours. Myriad entertainment providers now compete for our attention and that of young people in particular. The young are often left alone to try to find ways to avoid (or at least slow) this flood of customised content and entertainment services. Digital disconnection and 'digital-detox' are recommended in normative discourses, but considered old-fashioned or utopic by many young people (and even most of the adults around them). Entertainment in digital environments (the metaverse) requires further exploration and analysis. The issue is pressing in the light of the sizeable chunks of young people's lives being spent in these environments, the amount of attention and energy that is devoted to them and the influence that they have on consumption and travel choices and habits.

The (ab)use of social media is another critical issue in youth tourism. Young tourists were born and are growing up in an era disrupted by smartphones and have no memories of life without these pervasive and invasive devices. Worrying about creating social media content is time and energy-consuming and prevents us from actually living in the present moment. The discussion in Chapter 4 draws heavily on Shoshana Zuboff's (2019) brave and insightful volume *The Age of Surveillance Capitalism* and calls for caution in relation to the use of 'nudges' in tourism marketing. Zuboff (2019, p. 8) argues that

> surveillance capitalism unilaterally claims human experience as free raw material for translation into behavioural data. Although some of these data are applied to product and service improvement, the rest are [...] fabricated into *prediction products that anticipate what you will do now, soon and later.*

To be able to anticipate young tourists' behaviour, offer them personalised products and services and nudge them to consume is an extremely attractive proposition for many tourism marketers and service providers. Although it acknowledges the benefits of technological and digital innovation in youth tourism, the book's third contribution is its postulation that smartphones, social media and the metaverse limit young tourists' capacity to make independent decisions. Young people perceive their smartphones to be enablers and facilitators but also recognise that they can function as barriers between users and their immediate surroundings and thus obstacles to real immersion in tourism experiences. Little research has been done to date on either young tourists' attempts to overcome social media-induced FOMO (fear of missing out) or their experiences of the recently conceptualised JOMO (joy of missing out). This area is very likely to prove both fruitful and helpful.

Future Research Paths

One of the key issues in youth tourism today is sustainability. In October 2022, as I write these pages, the United Nations COP27 Conference on Climate Change is about to begin in Egypt. This book starts with a quotation from a speech by the UN Secretary-General António Guterres in which he makes it very clear that older generations are not accepting their responsibility for the extent to which their activities have caused and are exacerbating climate change and still seem to believe that the problem is the one to be dealt with by 'future' generations. Guterres (2022) told the terrifying truth: 'We are in a life-or-death struggle for our own safety today and *our survival tomorrow*'. He also pointed to our complete dereliction of duty, saying: 'while climate chaos gallops ahead, climate action has stalled'. I think that this is all very evident to many of the young, although perhaps less to the old. Children, adolescents and young adults have all been taught about the devastating effects of climate change and many, sadly, have direct experiences of it. Youth movements such as Fridays for Future show that young people do not accept the fact that they are being expected to deal with the environmental devastation that they have been bequeathed and did nothing to cause: sky-rocketing CO2 emissions, dying oceans, disappearing forests, etc. Young activists and protesters are urging governments, industries and 'adults' to take – immediate – concrete action to limit the (over)consumption of resources. The normative discourse on Action for Climate Empowerment on the United Nations' website (unfccc.int/ace), while addressing the role of governments and industries, nevertheless urges that: 'everyone, including and *perhaps especially the young*, *must understand and participate in* the transition to a low-emission, climate-resilient world'. The environmental harms of tourism are generally recognised in academia and there is a growing body of research calling for action and behavioural change. Education for sustainability in tourism (Moscardo & Benckendorff, 2015) and humanistic perspectives in tourism (Della Lucia & Giudici, 2021) suggest possible ways to shift this narrative, but further research and actions are needed. The Global Youth Summit (2022) was helpful in that it focused attention on young people, but future generations cannot be left to find practicable solutions to overtourism, overconsumption and the exploitation of the natural environment. Quite simply, this is not a matter for the future, but for today.

Future research on youth tourism should investigate the influence of online and blended education (study from home) on study abroad programs. How will the plethora of online learning opportunities influence the student tourism market? A work-life balance that enables people to travel has become important for the young, especially in this post-pandemic period. In future, will digital nomadism become a mainstream tourism activity? Digital nomads often participate in virtual communities of like-minded people to share experiences and give advice on where to go and what to do. Will this information exchange within virtual communities contribute to the creation of digital-nomad travel trajectories?

While this volume has looked in some detail at digital nomadism, much less space has been given to young people and place-specific employment abroad. Tourism and hospitality, however, depend on young people's labour in a myriad of roles and in different contexts (formal and informal), as tour guides, rickshaw drivers, ski or surf-instructors, etc. In a recent study, Robinson et al. (2019) explored the interdependencies of youth employment and tourism arguing that many tourism organisations rely on an accessible and flexible young workforce, and young people are often hired to enhance a service-provider's 'youthful look'. Further research into this topic might shed light on the reasons why an unusually large number of young people left jobs in tourism and hospitality during and after the pandemic. In a similar vein, the role of young and female entrepreneurs in tourism and hospitality also merits further research (Filimonau et al., 2022). Many companies that promote responsible tourism provide evidence of how they alleviate poverty, cut back emissions, achieve net-zero waste, use renewable resources, etc. Tourism entrepreneurs in some rural or mountain environments have fostered or even developed short supply chains to offer high quality, local and sustainable food and beverages (Kline et al., 2013; McGehee, 2012). Putting human dignity at the centre of tourism employment, responsible companies work with local communities and are committed to achieving gender and ethnic balance in their workforces (Della Lucia & Giudici, 2021). Sustainable, ethical and human-centred tourism businesses are already fostering a paradigm shift in tourism management and will certainly be the engines of future youth tourism.

References

Adams, D. (1979). *Hitchhiker's guide to the galaxy*. Pan Books.

Adams, K. (2016). Identity, tourism. In J. Jafari & H. Xiao (Eds.), *Encyclopedia of tourism*. Springer.

Agger, B. (2011). iTime: Labor and life in a smartphone era. *Time and Society, 20*(1), 119–136.

Ames, D. R., Rose, P., & Anderson, C. P. (2006). The NPI-16 as a short measure of narcissism. *Journal of Research in Personality, 40*(4), 440–450.

Andriotis, K. (2010). Heterotopic erotic oases: The public nude beach experience. *Annals of Tourism Research, 37*, 1076–1096.

Anime Industry Report. (2021). https://aja.gr.jp/english/japan-anime-data

Anschütz, S., & Mazzucato, V. (2022). Travel and personal growth: The value of visits to the country of origin for transnational migrant youth. *Compare: A Journal of Comparative and International Education*. https://doi.org/10.1080/03057925.2022.2036593

Arnett, J. J. (Ed.). (2016). *The Oxford handbook on emerging adulthood*. Oxford.

Atchley, R. C. (1993). Continuity theory and the evolution of activity in later adulthood. In J. Kelly (Ed.), *Activity and aging* (pp. 5–16). Sage.

Backer. E., Leisch, F., & Dolnicar, S. (2017). Visiting friends or relatives? *Tourism Management, 60*, 56–64.

Bagnoli, A. (2009). 'On an introspective journey'. Identities and travel in young people's lives. *European Societies, 11*(3), 325–345.

Bauman, Z. (2000). *Liquid modernity*. Polity Press.

Bauman, Z. (2007). *Consuming life*. Polity Press.

BBC. (2022). 'Situationships': Why Gen Z are embracing the grey area. www.bbc.com/worklife/article/20220831-situationships-why-gen-z-are-embracing-the-grey-area

Bejan, A. (2019). Why the days seem shorter as we get older. *European Review, 27*(2), 187–194.

Belk, R. W. (2018). Ownership: The extended-self and the extended object. In J. Peck & S. B. Shu (Eds.), *Psychological ownership and consumer behavior* (pp. 53–68). Springer.

Benckendorff, P., Moscardo, G., & Pendergast, D. (Eds.). (2010). *Tourism and generation Y*. CABI Publishing.

Bennett, M. (1986). A developmental approach to training for intercultural sensitivity. *International Journal of Intercultural Relations, 10*, 179–196.

Berdychevsky, L. (2017). Sexual health education for young tourists. *Tourism Management, 62*, 189–195.

Berdychevsky, L., & Gibson, H. (2015). Phenomenology of young women's sexual risk-taking in tourism. *Tourism Management, 46*, 299–310.

Berdychevsky, L., Gibson, H., & Poria, Y. (2013). Women's sexual behavior in tourism: Loosening the bridle. *Annals of Tourism Research, 42*, 65–85.

Bernardi, M. (2018). Millennials, sharing economy and tourism: The case of Seoul. *Journal of Tourism Futures, 4*(1), 43–56.

Bessant, J., Pickard, S., & Watts, R. (2020). Translating Bourdieu into youth studies. *Journal of Youth Studies, 23*(1), 76–92.

Bird, K., & Krüger, H. (2005). The secret of transitions: The interplay of complexity and reduction in life course analysis. In R. Levy, P. Ghisletta, J. M. Le Goff, D. Spini, & E. Widmer (Eds.), *Towards and interdisciplinary perspective on the life course* (pp. 173–194). Elsevier.

Blatt, K., & Gallagher, J. (2013). Mobile workforce: The rise of the mobilocracy. In P. Bruck & M. Rao (Eds.), *Global mobile: Applications and innovations for the worldwide mobile ecosystem* (pp. 275–292). Information Today, Inc.

Blatterer, H. (2010). The changing semantics of youth and adulthood. *Cultural Sociology, 4*(1), 63–79.

Bourdieu, P. (1986). The forms of capital. In J. G. Richardson (Ed.), *Handbook of theory and research for the sociology of capital* (pp. 241–258). Greenwood Press.

Buhalis, D., & Karatay, N. (2022). Mixed reality (MR) for generation Z in cultural heritage tourism towards metaverse. In J. L. Stienmetz, B. Ferrer-Rosell, & D. Massimo (Eds.), *Information and communication technologies in tourism 2022*. Springer, Cham. https://doi.org/10.1007/978-3-030-94751-4_2.

Buhalis, D., & Sinarta, Y. (2019). Real-time co-creation and nowness service: Lessons from tourism and hospitality. *Journal of Travel and Tourism Marketing, 36*(5), 563–582.

Cai, W. (2018). Donkey friends in Europe: A mobile ethnographic study in group orientation of Chinese outbound backpackers. In C. Khoo-Lattimore & L. Y. Chinao (Eds.), *Asian youth travellers. Insights and implications* (pp. 79–96). Springer.

Canavan, B. (2017). Narcissism normalisation: Tourism influences and sustainability implications. *Journal of Sustainable Tourism, 25*(9), 1322–1337.

Canosa, A., & Graham, A. (2022). Reimagining children's participation: A child rights informed approach to social justice in tourism. *Journal of Sustainable Tourism.* https://doi.org/10.1080/09669582.2022.2073448

Carr, N. (1998). The young tourist: A case of neglected research. *Progress in Tourism and Hospitality Research, 4*(4), 307–318.

Carr, N., & Berdychevsky, L. (Eds.). (2022). *Sex in tourism. Exploring the light and the dark.* Channel View Publications.

Carvalho, A. (2008). Media(ted) discourse and society: Rethinking the framework of critical discourse analysis. *Journalism Studies, 9*(2), 161–177.

Carvalho, I., Ramires, A., & Bakas, F. (2022). Who are the language tourists? A factor-cluster analysis based on language-related attitudes, beliefs, and travel outcomes. *International Journal of Tourism Research.* http://doi.org/10.1002/jtr.2559

Cavagnaro, E., Staffieri, S., & Postma, A. (2018). Understanding millennials' tourism experience: Values and meaning to travel as a key for identifying target clusters for youth (sustainable) tourism. *Journal of Tourism Futures, 4*(1), 31–42.

Chen, J.-S. (2007). A study of fan culture: Adolescent experiences with Animé/manga Doujinshi and Cosplay in Taiwan. *Visual Arts Research, 33*(1), 14–24.

Christou, P., Farmaki, A., Saveriades, A., & Georgiou, M. (2020). Travel selfies on social networks, narcissism and the "attraction shading effect". *Journal of Hospitality and Tourism Management, 43*, 289–293.

Cohen, E. (2022). Mass tourism and personal experiences. In R. Sharpley (Ed.) *Routledge handbook of the tourist experience* (pp. 235–248). Routledge.

Cohen, J. (2001). Defining identification: A theoretical look at the identification of audiences with media characters. *Mass Communication and Society, 4*(3), 245–264.

Cohen, S. (2011). Lifestyle travellers: Backpacking as a way of life. *Annals of Tourism Research, 38*(4), 1535–1555.

Cohen, S., Liu, H., Hanna, P., Hopkins, D., Higham, J., & Gössling, S. (2022). The Rich Kids on Instagram: Luxury travel, transport modes and desire. *Journal of Travel Research, 61*(7), 1479–1494.

Corbisiero, F. (2022). NetGen and tourism. In F. Corbisiero, S. Monaco, & E. Ruspini (Eds.), *Millennials, generation Z and the future of tourism* (pp. 47–82). Channel View Publications.

Corbisiero, F., & Ruspini, E. (2018). Millennials and generation Z: Challenges and future perspectives for international tourism. *Journal of Tourism Futures, 4*(1), 3–104.

Corbisiero, F., Monaco, S., & Ruspini, E. (2022). *Millennials, Generation Z and the future of tourism.* Channel View Publications.

Côté, J. (2014). *Youth studies: Fundamental issues and debates.* Palgrave Macmillan.

Cramer, P. (2011). Narcissism through the ages: What happens when narcissists grow older? *Journal of Research in Personality, 45,* 479–492.

De Jong, A. (2017). Unpacking pride's commodification through the encounter. *Annals of Tourism Research, 63,* 128–139.

De Mooij, M. (2019). *Consumer behavior and culture: Consequences for global marketing and advertising* (3rd ed.). Sage.

Della Lucia, M., & Giudici, E. (2021). Humanistic tourism. Exploring old and new tourism challenges from a humanistic perspective. In M. Della Lucia & E. Giudici (Eds.), *Humanistic tourism. Values, norms, and dignity* (pp. 1–14). Routledge.

Destatis. (2022). Number and proportion of young people aged between 15 and 24 years at all-time low. https://www.destatis.de/EN/Press/2022/07/PE22_N046_122.html

Diehl, K., & Zauberman, G. (2022). Capturing life or missing it: How mindful photo-taking can affect experiences. *Current Opinion in Psychology, 46,* 101334.

Dinholp, A., & Gretzel, U. (2016). Selfie-taking as touristic looking. *Annals of Tourism Research, 57,* 126–139.

du Bois-Reymond, M. (2015). Emerging adulthood theory and social class. In J. J. Arnett (Ed.), *The Oxford handbook of emerging adulthood* (pp. 47–61). Oxford.

Durkheim, É. [1912] 1995. *The elementary forms of the religious life.* The Free Press.

Dwivedi, Y. K., Hughes, L., Baabdullah, A. M., Ribeiro-Navarrete, S., Giannakis, M., Al-Debei, M. M., Dennehy, D., Metri, B., Buhalis, D., Cheung, C., Conboy, K., Doyle, R., Dubey, R., Dutot, V., Goyal, R. F., Gustafsson, A., Hinsch, C., Jebabli, I., Janssen, M., Kim, Y-G., Kim, J., Koos, S., Kreps, D., Kshetri, N., Kumar, V., Ooi, K-B, Papagiannidis, S., Pappas, I. O., Polyviou, A., Park, S-M., Pandey, N., Queiroz, M. M., Raman, R., Rauschnabel, P. A., Shirish, A., Sigala, M., Spanaki, K., Wei-Han Tan, G., Kumar Tiwari, M., Viglia, G., Fosso Wamba, S. (2022). Metaverse beyond the hype: Multidisciplinary perspectives on emerging challenges, opportunities, and agenda for research, practice and policy. *International Journal of Information Management, 66,* 102542. https://doi.org/10.1016/j.ijinfomgt.2022.102542

Eiser, J. R., & Ford, N. (1995). Sexual relationships on holiday: A case of situational disinhibition? *Journal of Social and Personal Relationships, 12*(3), 323–339.

Eurostat. *Population and demography.* www.ec.europa.eu/Eurostat

Everingham, P., Matthews, A., & Young, T. (2022). Embodying liminality: Exploring the 'affects' in sexual encounters in backpacker and volunteer tourism. In N. Carr & L. Berdychevsky (Eds.), *Sex in tourism. Exploring the light and the dark* (pp. 81–101). Channel View Publications.

Falk, J. H., Ballantyne, R., Packer, J., & Benckendorff, P. (2012). Travel and learning. A neglected tourism research area. *Annals of Tourism Research, 39*(2), 908–927.

Fan, D. X. F., Buhalis, D., & Lin, B. (2019). A tourist typology of online and face-to-face social contact: Destination immersion and tourism encapsulation/decapsulation. *Annals of Tourism Research, 78,* 102757.

Filimonau, V., Matyakubov, U., Matniyozov, M., Shaken, A., & Mika, M. (2022). Women entrepreneurs in tourism in a time of a life event crisis. *Journal of Sustainable Tourism.* https://doi.org/10.1080/09669582.2022.2091142

Foucault, M. (1986). Of other spaces. *Diacritics, 16,* 22–27.

Gardiner, S., King, B., & Wilkins, H. (2013). The travel behaviours of international students: Nationality-based constraints and opportunities. *Journal of Vacation Marketing, 19*(4), 290–294.

Ge, J., & Gretzel, U. (2018). Emoji rhetoric: A social media influencer perspective. *Journal of Marketing Management, 34*(15–16), 1272–1295.

Getz, D. (2008). Event tourism: Definition, evolution, and research. *Tourism Management, 29*(3), 403–428.

Gibson, H. J., & Yiannakis, A. (2002). Tourist roles: Needs and the life course. *Annals of Tourism Research, 29*, 358–383.

Goffman, E. (1959). *The presentation of self in everyday life.* Doubleday.

Graburn, N. (1983). The anthropology of tourism. *Annals of Tourism Research, 10*(1), 9–33.

Gray, H. P. (1970). *International travel—International trade.* Lexington Books.

Gretzel, U. (2018). Influencer marketing in travel and tourism. In M. Sigala & U. Gretzel (Eds.), *Advances in social media for travel, tourism and hospitality: New perspectives, practice and cases* (pp. 147–156). Routledge.

Gretzel, U., & Hardy, A. (2019). #VanLife: Materiality, makeovers and mobility amongst digital nomads, *e-Review of Tourism Research, 16*(2/3), 1–9.

Gretzel, U., & Yoo, K. H. (2008). Use and Impact of Online Travel Reviews. In O'Connor, P., Höpken, W., Gretzel, U. (Eds.), *Information and communication technologies in tourism 2008.* Springer, Vienna. https://doi.org/10.1007/978-3-211-77280-5_4

Guterres, A. (2019). *The climate emergency and the next generation.* https://www.un.org/sg/en/content/sg/articles/2019-03-15/the-climate-emergency-and-the-next-generation

Guterres, A. (2022). Secretary-General's opening remarks at press encounter on Pre-COP27.

Gyimóthy, S. (2018). Transformation in destination texture: Curry and Bollywood romance in the Swiss Alps. *Tourist Studies, 18*(3), 292–314.

Hajibaba, H., & Dolnicar, S. (2017). Substitutable by peer-to-peer accommodation networks? *Annals of Tourism Research, 66*, 185–188.

Hammer, M. R. (2013a). *A resource guide for effectively using the intercultural development inventory (IDI).* IDI, LLC.

Hammer, M. R., Bennett M. J., & Wiseman R. (2003). Measuring intercultural sensitivity: The intercultural development inventory. *International Journal of Intercultural Relations, 27*(3), 421–443.

Harris, L., O'Malley, L., & Story, V. (2022). Hens and stags. What happens in Barca stays in Barca. *Annals of Tourism Research, 92*, 103232.

Harris Poll. (2021). *The great awakening.* https://theharrispoll.com/the-great-awakening/

Hendin, H. M., & Cheek, J. M. (1997). Assessing hypersensitive narcissism: A re-examination of Murray's narcissism scale. *Journal of Research in Personality, 31*, 588–599.

Hermann, I., & Paris, C. M. (2020). Digital nomadism: The nexus of remote working and travel mobility. *Information Technology and Tourism, 22*, 329–334.

Heuman, D. (2005). Hospitality and reciprocity. Working tourists in Dominica. *Annals of Tourism Research, 32*(2), 407–418.

Hill, K. (2022). This is life in the metaverse. *The New York Times*, October 7. www.nytimes.com

Holt-Lunstad, J. (2022). Social connection as a public health issue: The evidence and a systemic framework for prioritizing the "social" in social determinants of health. *Annual Review of Public Health, 43*, 193–213.

Horton, D., & Wohl, R. R. (1956). Mass communication and parasocial interaction: Observations on intimacy at a distance. *Psychiatry,19*, 188–211.

Howe, N., & Strauss, W. (1991). *Generations: The history of America's Future, 1584 to 2069.* HarperCollins.

Hubbard, P. (2002). Sexing the self: Geographies of engagement and encounter. *Social and Cultural Geography, 3*(4), 365–381.

Irimiás, A., Csordás, T., Kiss, N., & Michalkó, G. (2021) Aggregated roles of smartphones in young adults' leisure and well-being: A diary study. *Sustainability*, *13*, 4133.

Irimiás A., & Franch, M. (2019) Developing intercultural sensitivity as an emotional ability. In E. Koc (Ed.), *Emotional intelligence in tourism and hospitality* (pp. 95–107). CABI.

Irimiás, A., Franch, M., & Mitev, A. (2020) Humanistic management training: An explorative study on Erasmus students' intercultural sensitivity. In M. Della Lucia & E. Giudici (Eds.), *Shaping a humanistic perspective for the tourism industry* (pp. 128–146). Routledge.

Irimiás, A., & Mitev, A. (2021a). Lockdown captivity: The wish to break out and travel. *Current Issues in Tourism*, *24*(19), 2706–2709.

Irimiás, A., & Mitev, A. (2023). Tourists as caged birds: Elaborating travel thoughts and craving when feeling captive. *Journal of Travel Research*, *62*(1), 91–104. https://doi.org/10.1177/0047287521105668

Irimiás, A., Mitev, A., & Michalkó, G. (2018). Voices of the fisher king: Narratives of older travellers' religious journeys. *Journal of Global Scholars of Marketing Science*, *28*(3), 221–238.

Irimiás, A., Mitev, A., & Michalkó, G. (2021). Narrative transportation and travel: The mediating role of escapism and immersion. *Tourism Management Perspectives*, *38*, 100793.

Jackson, J. (2015). Becoming interculturally competent: Theory to practice in international education. *International Journal of Intercultural Relations*, *48*, 91–107.

Jakab, G., Szalai, Z., Michalkó, G., Ringer, M., Filep, T., Szabó, L., Maász, G., Pirger, Z., Ferincz, Á., Staszny, Á., Dobosy, P. & Kondor, A. C. (2020). Thermal baths as sources of pharmaceutical and illicit drug contamination. *Environmental Science and Pollution Research*, *27*, 399–410.

Jensen, M., Gyimóthy, S., & Jensen, O. B. (2016). Staging interrail mobilities. *Tourist Studies*, *16*(2), 111–132.

Jenson, J. (1992). Fandom as pathology: The consequences of characterization. In L. A. Lewis (Ed.), *The adoring audience. Fan culture and popular media* (pp. 67–88). Routledge.

Johnson, S. K., Goldman, J. A., Garey, A. I., Britner, P. A., & Weaver, S. E. (2011). Emerging adults' identity exploration: Illustrations from inside the "Camp Bubble". *Journal of Adolescent Research*, *26*(2), 258–295.

Jones, A. (2004). *Review of gap year provision.* Department of Education and Skills.

Ketter, E. (2021). Millennial travel: Tourism micro-trends of European Generation Y. *Journal of Tourism Futures*, *7*(2), 192–196.

Khoo-Lattimore, C., & Yang, E. C. L. (Eds.). (2018). *Asian youth travellers. Insights and implications.* Springer.

Kirillova, K., Lehto, X., & Cai, L. (2015). Volunteer tourism and intercultural sensitivity: The role of interaction with host communities. *Journal of Travel and Tourism Marketing*, *32*, 382–400.

Kirillova, K., Peng, C., & Cheng, H. (2019). Anime consumer motivation for anime tourism and how to harness it. *Journal of Travel and Tourism Marketing*, *36*(2), 268–281.

Kline, C., McGehee, N., Paterson, S., & Tsao, J. (2013). Using ecological systems theory and density acquaintance to explore resident perception of entrepreneurial climate. *Journal of Travel Research*, *52*(3), 294–309.

Kock, F., Josiassen, A., & Assaf, A. G. (2018). On the origin of tourist behaviour. *Annals of Tourism Research,73*, 180–183.

Kock, F., Josiassen, A., Assaf, A. G., Karpen, I., & Farrelly, F. (2019). Tourism ethnocentrism and its effects on tourist and resident behavior. *Journal of Travel Research*, *58*(3), 429–439.

Koo, C., Kwon, J., Chung, N., & Kim, J. (2022). Metaverse tourism: Conceptual framework and research propositions. *Current Issues in Tourism*. https://doi.org/10.1080/13683 500.2022.2122781

Le Bigot, J.-Y., Lott-Vernet, C., & Mukherjee, P. (2007). Youth research. In M. van Hamersveld & C. de Bont (Eds.), *Market research handbook* (5th ed., pp. 283–297). John Wiley & Sons, Ltd.

Lehto, X., Jang, S., Achana, F. T., & O'Leary, J. T. (2008). Exploring tourism experience sought: A cohort comparison of Baby Boomers and the Silent Generation. *Journal of Vacation Marketing, 14*(3), 237–252.

Lejealle, C., King, B., & Chapuis, J. M. (2021). Decoding the educational travel decision: Destinations, institutions and social influence. *Current Issues in Tourism, 21*(24), 3107–3120.

Lewis, C., Nelson, K., & Black, R. (2021). Moving millennials out of the too hard basket: Exploring the challenges of attracting millennial tourists to rural destinations. *Journal of Hospitality and Tourism Management, 46*, 96–103.

Liu, H., Wu, L., & Li, X. (2019). Social media envy: How experience sharing on social networking sites drives millennials' aspirational tourism consumption. *Journal of Travel Research, 58*(3), 355–369.

Liu, S., Lai, D., Huang, S., & Li, Z. (2021). Scale development and validation of anime tourism motivations. *Current Issues in Tourism, 24*(20), 2939–2954.

Liu, Y. (2019). *Millennials' attitudes towards influencer marketing and purchase intentions*. California State University.

Lovell, J., & Thurgill, J. (2021). Extending hot authentication: Imagining fantasy space. *Annals of Tourism Research, 84*, 103134.

MacCannell, D. (2002). *The tourist. A new theory of the leisure class*. University of California Press.

Magasic, M., & Gretzel, U. (2020). Travel connectivity. *Tourist Studies, 20*(1), 3–26.

Makimoto, T., & Manners, D. (1997). *Digital nomad*. Wiley.

Manka, M. (2022). Interrail youth travel (re)producing communities of belonging – Memories of Finnish travellers 1972–1991. *Journal of Tourism History*. https://doi. org/10.1080/1755182X.2022.2065366

Marin, J., Grijalvo, M., & Mundet, L. (2021). Can a mature sun and beach tourist destination change its image among tourists in Lloret de Mar, Spain? *Tourism, 69*(4), 527–542.

Martins, M. R., & Costa, R. A. (2022). *The backpacker tourist: A contemporary perspective*. Emerald Publishing Limited.

Mason, A., Lee, R., &Members of the NTA Network. (2022). Six ways population change will affect the global economy. *Population and Development Review*. https://doi. org/10.1111/padr.12469

McCrindle Research. (2020). *Understanding generation alpha*. https://mccrindle.com.au/ article/topic/generation-alpha/generation-alpha-defined/

McGehee, N. G. (2012). Oppression, emancipation and volunteer tourism. Research propositions. *Annals of Tourism Research, 39*(1), 84–107.

McGehee, N. G., & Andereck, K. (2009). Volunteer tourism and the 'voluntoured': The case of Tijuana, Mexico. *Journal of Sustainable Tourism, 17*(1), 39–51.

McGehee, N. G., & Santos, C. A. (2005). Social change, discourse and volunteer tourism. *Annals of Tourism Research, 32*(3), 760–779.

McKercher, B., & Bauer, T. G. (2003). Conceptual framework of the nexus between tourism, romance, and sex. In T. G. Bauer & B. McKercher (Eds.), *Sex and tourism: Journeys of romance, love, and lust* (pp. 3–17). Haworth Hospitality Press.

McLeay, F., Lichy, J., & Major, B. (2019). Co-creation of the ski-chalet community experiencescape. *Tourism Management, 74*, 413–424.

Michalkó, G. (2022). *A turizmus esszenciája*. Akadémiai Kiadó.

Migacz, S. J., & Petrick, J. F. (2018). Millennials: America's cash cow is not necessarily a herd. *Journal of Tourism Futures, 4*(1), 16–30.

Mitev, A. (2007a). A narrative analysis of university students' alcohol stories in terms of a Fryeian framework. *European Journal of Mental Health, 2*(2), 205–233.

Mitev, A. (2007b). Egyetemisták alkoholtörténeteinek strukturális elemzése. *Addiktológia: Addictologia Hungarica, 6*(1), 19–38.

Mitev, A., & Irimiás, A. (2021). Travel craving. *Annals of Tourism Research, 90,* 103111.

Moscardo, G., & Benckendorff, P. (Eds.). (2015). *Education for sustainability in tourism.* Springer.

Nagy, G. (2016). Youth hostel parents in Germany. *Annals of Tourism Research, 57,* 234–278.

Neuhofer, B., Egger, R., Yu, J., & Celuch, K. (2021). Designing experiences in the age of human transformation: An analysis of Burning Man. *Annals of Tourism Research, 91,* 103310.

Noy, C., & Cohen, E. (2005). *Israeli backpackers. From tourism to rite of passage.* State University of New York Press.

O'Reilly, C. C. (2006). From drifter to gap year tourist. Mainstreaming backpacker travel. *Annals of Tourism Research, 33*(4), 998–1017.

OECD. (2021). *Indicator B6. What is the profile of internationally mobile students?* https://www.oecd-ilibrary.org/sites/5a49e448-en/index.html?itemId=/content/component/5a49e448-en

Olsen, D. H. (2022). Religious tourism: A spiritual or touristic experience? In R. Sharpley (Ed.), *The Routledge handbook on the tourist experience* (pp. 391–407). Routledge.

Olson, L. C., & Kroeger, K. R. (2001). Global competency and intercultural sensitivity. *Journal of Studies in International Education, 5*(2), 116–137.

Oxford English Dictionary Online. (2022). www.oed.com

Paulsen, J., Syed, M., Trzesniewski, K., & Donnellan, M. B. (2015). Generational perspectives on emerging adulthood: A focus on narcissism. In J. J. Arnett (Ed.) *The Oxford handbook on emerging adulthood* (pp. 26–44). Oxford University Press.

Pearce, P. L. (2005). *Tourist behaviour. Themes and conceptual schemes.* Channel View Publications.

Pearce, P. L. (2011). *Tourist behaviour and the contemporary world.* Channel View Publications.

Pearce, P. L. (2022). The Ulysses factor revisited. Consolidating the travel career pattern approach to tourist motivation. In R. Sharpley (Ed.) *The Routledge handbook on the tourist experience* (pp. 169–184). Routledge.

Pearce, P. L., & Coghlan, A. (2008). The dynamics behind volunteer tourism. In S. Wearing & K. Lyons (Eds.), *Journeys of discovery in volunteer tourism: International case study perspectives.* CABI.

Pearce P. L., & Foster F. (2007). A "University of Travel": Backpacker learning. *Tourism Management, 28*(5), 1285–1298.

Petry, T., Pikkemaat, B., Chan, C. S., & Scholl-Grissemann, U. (2022). Understanding students as hosts: Moving beyond sightseeing. *International Journal of Culture, Tourism and Hospitality Research, 16*(1), 7–19.

Pew Research Center. (2019). Where millennials end and generation Z begins. https://www.pewresearch.org/fact-tank/2019/01/17/where-millennials-end-and-generation-z-begins/

Pew Research Center. (2020). On the cusp of adulthood and facing an uncertain future: What we know about gen Z so far. https://www.pewresearch.org/social-trends/2020/05/14/on-the-cusp-of-adulthood-and-facing-an-uncertain-future-what-we-know-about-gen-z-so-far-2/

Pew Research Center. (2021) Teens, social media and technology. https://www.pewresearch.org/internet/2022/08/10/teens-social-media-and-technology-2021/

Pew Research Center. (2022). Financial issues top the list of reasons U.S. adults live in multigenerational homes. https://www.pewresearch.org/social-trends/2022/03/24/financial-issues-top-the-list-of-reasons-u-s-adults-live-in-multigenerational-homes/

Polus, R., & Carr, N. (2022). From genXers to millennials. Transformation of self through tourism. In S. K. Walia & A. Jasrotia (Eds.), *Millennials, spirituality and tourism* (pp. 201–216). Routledge.

Pop, N. A., Stăncioiu, F. A., Onișor, L.-F., Baba, C. A., & Anysz, R. N. (2022). Exploring the attitude of youth towards adventure tourism as a driver for post-pandemic era tourism experiences. *Current Issues in Tourism*. https://doi.org/10.1080/13683500.2022.2049712

Povilaitis, V., & Tamminen, K. A. (2018). Delivering positive youth development at a residential summer sport camp. *Journal of Adolescent Research*. https://doi.org/10.1177/0743558417702478

Prentice, R. (2004). Tourist motivation and typologies. In A. A. Lew, M. C. Hall, & A. M. Williams (Eds.), *A companion to tourism* (pp. 261–279). Blackwell Publishing.

Pritchard, A., & Morgan, N. (2006). Hotel Babylon? Exploring hotels as liminal sites of transition and transgression. *Tourism Management*, *27*, 762–772.

Ralston, R., Lumsdon, L., & Downward, P. (2005). The third force in events tourism: Volunteers at the XVII Commonwealth games. *Journal of Sustainable Tourism*, *13*(5), 504–519.

Reijnders, S. (2021). *Places of imagination. Media, tourism, culture.* Ashgate Publishing.

Reisinger, Y., & Turner, L. (2011). *Cross-cultural behaviour in tourism: Concepts and analysis.* Routledge.

Rexeisen, R. J., Anderson, P. H., Lawton, L., & Hubbard, A. C. (2008). Study abroad and intercultural development: A longitudinal study. Frontiers. *The Interdisciplinary Journal of Study Abroad*, *17*, 1–20.

Richards, G. (2015). The new global nomads: Youth travel in a globalizing world. *Tourism Recreation Research*, *40*(3), 340–352.

Richards, G., & Morrill, W. (2020). Motivations of global millennial travelers. *Revista Brasileira dePesquisa em Turismo*, *14*(1), 126–139.

Richards, G., & Wilson, J. (2004). The international student travel market: Travel style, motivations, and activities. *Tourism Review International*, *8*(2), 57–67.

Richards, G., & Wilson, J. (2005). Youth tourism. Finally coming of age? In M. Novelli (Ed.) *Niche tourism. Contemporary issues, trends and cases* (pp. 39–46). Elsevier Butterworth-Heinemann.

Ritchie, B., Carr, N., & Cooper, C. (2003). *Managing educational tourism.* Channel View Publications.

Robinson, R. N. S., Baum, T., Golubovskaya, M., Solnet, D. J., & Callan, V. (2019). Applying endosymbiosis theory: Tourism and its young workers. *Annals of Tourism Research*, *78*, 102751.

Ruspini, E. (2022). Generations, events, experiences and tourism. In F. Corbisiero, S. Monaco, & E. Ruspini (Eds.), *Millennials, Generation Z and the future of tourism* (pp. 3–25). Channel View Publications.

Russell, C. A., & Stern, B. B. (2006). Consumers, characters, and products: A balance model of sitcom product placement effects. *Journal of Advertising*, *35*(1), 7–21.

Sarman, I., Scagnolari, S., & Maggi, R. (2016). Acceptance of life-threatening hazards among young tourists: A stated choice experiment. *Journal of Travel Research*, *55*(8), 979–992.

Schänzel, H. A., Yeoman, I., & Backer, E. (2012). *Family tourism: Multidisciplinary perspectives.* Channel View Publications.

Schiappa, E., Allen, M., & Gregg, P. B. (2007). Parasocial relationships and television: A meta-analysis of the effects. In R. Preiss, B. Gayle, N. Burrell, M. Allen, & J. Bryant

(Eds.), *Mass media effects research: Advances through meta-analysis* (pp. 301–314). Erlbaum.

Selänniemi, T. (2003). On holiday in the liminoid playground: Place, time, and self in tourism. In T. G. Bauer & B. McKercher (Eds.), *Sex and tourism: Journeys of romance, love, and lust* (pp. 19–31). Haworth Hospitality Press.

Selby, M. (2021). Mobile student experience: The place of tourism. *Annals of Tourism Research, 90*, 103253.

Shaftel, J., Shaftel, T., & Ahluwalia, R. (2007). International educational experience and intercultural competence. *Journal of Business & Economics, 6*(1), 25–34.

Sharpley, R. (2018). *Tourism, tourists and society* (5th ed.). Routledge.

Sharpley, R. (2021). Tourist experiences: Liminal, liminoid or just doing something different? In R. Sharpley (Ed.), *The Routledge handbook on the tourist experience* (pp. 89–100). Routledge.

Shaw, G., & Williams, A. M. (2004). *Tourism and tourism spaces.* SAGE Publications.

Sigala, M. (2012). Introduction to Chapter 1. In M. Sigala, E. Christou, & U. Gretzel (Eds.), *Social media in travel, tourism and hospitality* (pp. 7–10). Ashgate.

Sigala, M., Christou, E., &Gretzel, U. (Eds.). (2012). *Social media in travel, tourism and hospitality: Theory, practice and cases.* Ashgate.

Skinner, H., Sarpong, D., & White, G. R. (2018). Meeting the needs of the millennials and generation Z: Gamification in tourism through geocaching. *Journal of Tourism Futures, 4*(1), 93–104.

Sönmez, S., Apostolopoulos, Y., Theocharous, A., & Massengale, K. (2013). Bar crawls, foam parties, and clubbing networks: Mapping the risk environment of a Mediterranean nightlife resort. *Tourism Management Perspectives, 8*, 49–59.

St John, G. (2018). Civilised tribalism: Burning Man, event-tribes and maker culture. *Cultural Sociology, 12*(1), 3–21.

Statista. (2020). *Tourism worldwide.* https://www.statista.com/outlook/mmo/travel-tourism/worldwide

Statista. (2022). *Industries & Markets. US Millennial travel.* https://www.statista.com/study/58457/millennial-travel-behavior/

Statista. (2022a). *Number of Netflix paid subscribers worldwide from 1st quarter 2013 to 3rd quarter 2022.* https://www.statista.com/statistics/250934/quarterly-number-of-netflix-streaming-subscribers-worldwide/

Statista. (2022b). *Anime industry in Japan - statistics and facts.* https://www.statista.com/topics/7495/anime-industry-in-japan/

Steinecke, A. (2016). *Filmtourismus.* UVK.

Stephenson, N. (1992). *Snow crash.* Bantam Books.

Stone, M. J., & Petrick, J. F. (2013). The educational benefits of travel experiences: A literature review. *Annals of Tourism Research, 52*(6), 731–744.

Strauss, W., & Howe, N. (1991). *Generations: The history of America's future.* Quill.

Stryker, S., & Burke, P. J. (2000). The past, present and future of identity theory. *Social Psychology Quarterly, 63*, 284–297.

Tan, W.-K., & Yang, C.-Y. (2021). The relationship between narcissism and landmark check-in behaviour on social media. *Current Issues in Tourism, 24*, 3489–3507.

Thaler, R. H., & Sunstein, C. R. (2009). *Nudge: Improving decisions about health, wealth and happiness.* Penguin Books.

Threadgold, S. (2019). Figures of youth: On the very object of youth studies. *Journal of Youth Studies, 23*(6), 686–701.

Timothy, D. J., & Olsen, D. H. (2006). *Tourism, religion and spiritual journeys.* Routledge.

Timothy, D. J., & Zhu, X. (2022). Backpacker tourist experiences. Temporal, spatial and cultural perspectives. In R. Sharpley (Ed.), *The Routledge handbook on the tourist experience* (pp. 249–261). Routledge.

Triandis, H. (2006). Cultural intelligence in organizations. *Group and Organization Management*, *31*(1), 20–26.

Tung, V. W. S., Lee, S., & Hudson, S. (2019). The potential of anime for destination marketing: Fantasies, otaku and the kidult segment. *Current Issues in Tourism*, *22*(12), 1423–1436.

Tussyadiah, I. P., & Wang, D. (2016). Tourists' attitudes towards proactive smartphone systems. *Journal of Travel Research*, *55*(4), 493–508.

Twenge, J. M. (2006). *Generation me: Why today's young Americans are more confident, assertive, entitled and more miserable than ever before*. Free Press.

Twenge, J. M., & Hamilton, J. L. (2022). Linear correlation is insufficient as the sole measure of associations: The case of technology use and mental health. *Acta Psychologica*, *229*, 103696.

United Nations. (2022). *The sustainable development goals reports*. unstats.un.org/sdgs/report/2022/

UNWTO. (2016). Affiliate members global reports. *Global report on the power of youth travel*, Vol. *13*: The power of youth travel. Madrid.

Urry, J. (1994). Cultural change and contemporary tourism. *Leisure Studies*, *13*, 233–238.

Volo, S. (2021). Tourist experience: A marketing perspective. In: R. Sharpley (Ed.), *Routledge handbook of the tourist experience* (pp. 549–563). Routledge.

Volo, S., & Irimiás, A. (2021). Instagram: Visual methods in tourism research. *Annals of Tourism Research*, *91*, 103093.

Volo, S., & Irimiás, A. (2022). Consumer behavior in e-Tourism. In Z. Xiang, M. Fuchs, U. Gretzel, & W. Höpken (Eds.), *Handbook of e-tourism*. Springer, Cham. https://doi.org/10.1007/978-3-030-05324-6_8-1

Wang, D., & Fesenmaier, D. (2013). Transforming the travel experience: The use of smartphones for travel. In L. Cantoni & Z. Xiang (Eds.), *Information and communication technologies in tourism* (pp. 58–69). Springer.

Wang, W., Yi, L., Wu, M. Y., Pearce, P. L., & Huang, S. S. (2018). Examining Chinese adult children's motivations for travelling with their parents. *Tourism Management*, *69*, 422–433.

Wearing, S. (2001). *Volunteer tourism: Experiences that make a difference*. CAB International.

Wearing, S., & McGehee, N. (2013). Volunteer tourism: A review. *Tourism Management*, 120–130. https://doi.org/10.1016/j.tourman.2013.03.002

Wearing, S., Mostafanezhad, M., Nguyen, N., Nguyen, T. H. T., & McDonald, M. (2018). 'Poor children on Tinder' and their Barbie Saviours: Towards a feminist political economy of volunteer tourism. *Leisure Studies*, *37*(5), 500–514.

Webster, D., Dunne, L., & Hunter, R. (2021). Association between social networks and subjective well-being in adolescents: A systematic review. *Youth & Society*, *53*(2), 175–210.

Webster, S. (2012). Consumer kids and tourists – Creatively marketing a city to young tourists. In H. Schänzel, I. Yeoman, & E. Backer (Eds.), *Family tourism. Multidisciplinary perspectives* (pp. 143–155). Channel View Publications.

Weiler, B., Gstaettner, A. M., & Scherrer, P. (2021). Selfies to die for: A review of research on self-photography associated with injury/death in tourism and recreation. *Tourism Management Perspectives*, *37*, 100778.

Wheatley, D., & Buglass, S. L. (2019). Social network engagement and subjective wellbeing: A life-course perspective. *British Journal of Sociology*, *70*(5), 1971–1995.

Williams, K. C., & Page, R. A. (2011). Marketing to the generations. *Journal of Behavioural Studies in Business*, *3*(3), 1–17.

Woods, O., & Shee, S. Y. (2021). "Doing it for the 'gram'"?The representational politics of popular humanitarianism. *Annals of Tourism Research*, *87*, 103107.

Woodside, A. G., & Megehee, C. M. (2010). Advancing consumer behaviour theory in tourism via visual narrative art. *International Journal of Tourism Research*, *12*, 418–431.

World Economic Forum. (2021). Davos Lab: Youth recovery plan. *Insight Report*. https://www.weforum.org/reports/youth-recovery-plan

World Health Organisation. (2021) *The global health observatory*. https://www.who.int/data/gho/data/themes/topics/topic-details/GHO/world-health-statistics

World Population Prospects. (2019). https://population.un.org/wpp/Download/Standard/Population/ (www.weforum.org)

World Youth Student & Educational Travel Confederation (WYSE, 2019). New Horizons IV: Multicountry trips in the European youth travel market. Amsterdam WYSE Travel Confederation.

Wu, M. Y., & Pearce P. L. (2018). Gap time and Chinese tourists: Exploring constraints. *Current Issues in Tourism*, *21*(10), 1171–1186.

Wu, M. Y., Pearce, P. L., Huang, K., & Fan, T. (2015). 'Gap Year' in China: Views from the participants and implications for the future. *Current Issues in Tourism*, *18*(2), 158–174.

Wu, S., & Dai, G. (2018). Heterotopia: A study on the spatial practice of Midi Music Festival. *Human Geography*, *33*(161), 49–56.

Wu, S., Li, Y., Wood, E. H., & Senaux, B. (2020). Liminality and festivals – Insights from the East. *Annals of Tourism Research*, *80*, 102810.

Wu, S., Li, Y., Wood, E. H., Senaux, B., & Dai, G. (2020). Liminality and festivals: Insights from the East. *Annals of Tourism Research*, *80*, 102810.

www.animecon.com

www.un.org/sg/en/content/sg/speeches/2022-10-03/secretary-generals-opening-remarks-press-encounter-pre-cop27

WYSE. (2021). *The power of youth travel*. https://www.wysetc.org/research/the-power-of-youth-travel/

Xiang, Z., & Gretzel, U. (2010). Role of social media in online travel information search. *Tourism Management*, *31*, 179–188.

Xie, J. (2022). *Understanding young Chinese backpackers. The pursuit of freedom and its risks*. Routledge.

Yamamura, T., & Seaton, P. (2020). *Contents tourism and pop culture fandom. Transnational tourist experiences*. Channel View Publications.

Zhang, J., Morrison, A. M., & Wu, B. C. (2018). Am I a backpacker? Factors indicating the social identity of Chinese backpackers. *Journal of Travel Research*, *57*(4), 525–539.

Zuboff, S. (2019). *The age of surveillance capitalism. The fight for a human future at the new frontier of power*. Profile Books.

Index

Printed in the United States
by Baker & Taylor Publisher Services